100 Years of Danish Modern

100 Years of Danish Modern

Vilhelm Lauritzen Architects

Christian Bundegaard

PUBLISHED WITH GENEROUS SUPPORT FROM

 DREYERSFOND

Hoffmann og
Husmans Fond

POLITIKEN-**FONDEN**

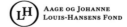 AAGE OG JOHANNE
LOUIS-HANSENS FOND

Table of contents

Buildings in motion

A late-summer night's adventure

Even the sleepiest dog walker would have sprung wide awake in an instant if they had been close enough to Copenhagen Airport in the early hours of Sunday, 19 September 1999.

Rolling along the runways was a vehicle so remarkable that observers from the Guinness Book of World Records were present to watch patiently as it covered a distance of just under four kilometres at a snail's pace. The slow rate of progress was necessary. The vehicle weighed 2,600 tons, was 110 metres long and had no fewer than 744 independent wheels to coordinate. Along the route, blasting experts with dynamite stood ready to blow up the contraption if something went awry, lest the peculiar construction get in the way of the first morning flights. However, the operation was accomplished right on time, and the Guinness representatives

The Vilhelm Lauritzen Terminal (1939) at Copenhagen Airport is one of the world's first airport terminals and one of the earliest examples of Nordic modernism.

were able to hand Copenhagen Airport the diploma for the largest building relocation project in the Europe.

The strange contraption was in fact a building going for a night-time drive. Over the years, the building had been subjected to heavy wear and tear as well as extensions with little respect for the architectural concept. It no longer looked its best; moreover, it was directly in the way of plans to expand the airport. The relocation and restoration cost the airport 100 million kroner (almost 13.5 million euros).

But what work of architecture could possibly be so special and worthy of preservation that it was transported like a princess on a pea, perched on a waterbed-like construction of linked-up trucks, after 400 precious building components had been carefully removed only to be meticulously restored to their place once the building arrived at its new foundation?

The answer is architect Vilhelm Lauritzen's airport terminal from 1939, which – to quote the airport's former director Niels Boserup – is 'one of the most significant manifestations of European modernism – a masterpiece'.[1] But who is this Lauritzen, who to anyone other than architecture aficionados might only be slightly better known than his faded masterpiece?

Vilhelm Lauritzen (1894–1984) is one of the most important figures of Danish modern architecture. Among other accomplishments, he and his architecture firm have designed several generations of buildings for Copenhagen Airport and for the national broadcasting corporation Danmarks Radio. He was a contemporary of Alvar Aalto, Arne Jacobsen and Poul Henningsen (PH), and, like his perhaps better-known colleagues, he has had a crucial impact on the development of the particular Nordic version of international modernism in architecture and design, which remains as vital as ever and continues to influence design, culture and societies in the Nordic region and the rest of the world.

Watercolour by Vilhelm Lauritzen from his proposal for the 1936 competition for the airport's first terminal. Lauritzen won the contract in competition with Arne Jacobsen, among others.

The anniversary of modern architecture

The architecture firm that carries his name has now been active for a hundred years without interruption and is currently headed by a fourth-generation partner collective.[2] Vilhelm Lauritzen Architects was founded the same year as Aalto's architecture practice and is of approximately the same vintage as the Bauhaus school, Le Corbusier's manifesto and the Barcelon a pavilion. This makes the firm about as old as modern architecture itself. It also belongs to the same generation as the Scandinavian welfare society, whose particular combination of social safety net and spiritual and economic liberalism has in recent years become an international social model.

Both these connections are worth bearing in mind as we celebrate the centenary. Throughout the so-called modern era, architecture and social development have mutually influenced each other – not always intentionally but certainly actively and sometimes proactively – to a higher degree than ever before in the history of the world. And despite certain setbacks, this era is far from over.

Modern architecture reflects the human need for constant renewal and development, the need to avoid settling into established norms and forms and to remain in motion. Just like the state of modern society, which requires us constantly to keep up with changing times and conditions. Conditions change, and today architecture is, not least, an applied art. Any architectural assignment must be addressed with consideration for the building's users and their needs, both of which might change repeatedly over the course of the building's lifetime.

Only architects consistently refer to even long-since completed buildings as 'projects'. Probably because they know that this is exactly what modern buildings are.

Architecture, which was once intended as a permanent temple to the building client, is now a project defined by rationality, needs analyses, user friendliness, humanism, efficiency, flexibility, sustainability, trends, public utility and numerous other factors. However, it is also a work of applied art, and thus, just as the application influences artistic decision, the reverse is also true: art – the design or tectonics – also defines and enables the application.

The handling of space, statics, scale, influx of light, material properties, siting and so forth has a direct impact on the functionality of the built structure as well as its aesthetic expression. In today's tightly planned construction processes, architects 'never sit around painting watercolours anymore', as one of the partners in Vilhelm Lauritzen Architects put it, but the skill and creative drive that characterize art are still architecture's raison d'être. This is also true of a modern and contemporary firm such as Vilhelm Lauritzen Architects.

Throughout the 1970s and 1980s, most of the firm's projects were based on commissions from two regular clients: Danmarks Radio and Copenhagen Airport. However, from the late 1980s, both began to engage with a broader range of architects. This might have spelled the end for the firm, but instead it inspired it to reinvent itself as a participant in both public and invited architecture competitions.

The company was expanded with employees dedicated to competition projects, three of whom later became partners. With this

Alvar Aalto's Heilig-Geist-Kirche (Church of the Holy Spirit) (1962) in Wolfsburg has several features in common with his Nordjyllands Kunstmuseum (North Jutland Art Museum), now Kunsten Museum of Modern Art Aalborg. Both buildings were designed in 1958.

Modern form: undecorated, plain white surfaces, flat roofs, straight angles and horizontal lines as in Mediterranean or traditional Arabic architecture. Shown here are the teachers' residences at the Bauhaus, designed by Walter Gropius.

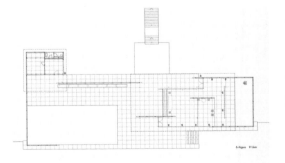

The modern spatial revolution: open-plan designs and the poetry of precision in Mies van der Rohe's design of the German contribution to the 1929 Barcelona International Exposition.

Copenhagen Business School
(2000) on Solbjerg Plads
in Frederiksberg is one of
Denmark's eight universities.
It has 20,000 students and
1,500 employees.

Following spread:
Concentration, professionalism,
communication and transparency are important architectural virtues. Here they are
manifested in Vilhelm Lauritzen
Architects' own offices.

new focus, the firm took part in the competitions for a concert hall
in Copenhagen (1994) and the offices of the Danish Association of
Architects, Arkitekternes Hus (Architects' House), in Strandgade
in Copenhagen (1994), but the breakthrough came in 1994 when it
won the contract for a new business school in Frederiksberg (now
Copenhagen Business School). That provided the necessary confidence, skills and resources to revitalize the studio. Aiming for a more
proactive pursuit of commissions and putting together the right
team for a given competition proved an energizing challenge.

Today, there is no doubt at Vilhelm Lauritzen Architects that
this 'reinvention' of the firm at a critical juncture boosted its internal confidence and professional profile and remains an important
daily motivation.

Address:
Nordhavn, Copenhagen,
the Danish welfare society

From the windows of the studio, on the first floor of a converted warehouse on a pier in Copenhagen's Nordhavn (North Harbour) district,
employees of Vilhelm Lauritzen Architects can keep an eye on no
fewer than three of their projects currently under construction. On a
clear day, they would almost be able to conduct site supervision from
behind their desks. From the balcony, where they have lunch in the
summertime, they can see three more, completed, buildings. All six
buildings are within a few hundred metres from the office.

Being a 'local' architect holds many advantages. Today, a major
building project is a complicated affair that involves numerous people, countless details and tight schedules. Local insight and a constant presence throughout the process are often crucial. That is why
architects working abroad almost always establish an on-site office,
unless they have a local partner. Personal presence matters. Enter-
ing the studio, one sees everyone hunched over their computers, just
as architects once sat stooped over the drawing table. However, that
first impression is deceiving. Their work is very tangible. Suddenly
one day, it is out there, part of the reality we all live in every day.

In marking the anniversary of the firm by telling its story, it
seems apt to focus on that reality – on the interaction between modern architecture and the modern Danish society in which buildings,
urban plans and design objects have taken shape.

It is a story about the construction of the welfare society as reflected in its tangible architecture. About buildings and social structures in motion. Since Vilhelm Lauritzen Architects has been part
of this journey from the early beginnings of modern architecture,
the firm's works and practice provide the story's main theme and
perspective.

In the following, presentations of the firm's works alternate with sections on the intellectual history of modernity with an emphasis on Danish conditions.

Chapter 1 deals with modernity as project, utopia and social experiment and with the qualities of humanism and sustainability that Vilhelm Lauritzen Architects seeks to incorporate into the built environment through a broad approach that includes user involvement, contextualism and designing for the human scale.

Chapter 2 outlines the development of the welfare society, from social reforms to environmental awareness and participatory democracy, and discusses Vilhelm Lauritzen Architects' commitment to giving architecture a meaningful social profile that is increasingly integrated into the design expression.

Chapter 3 examines Vilhelm Lauritzen Architects' contribution to preserving modern architecture's core concept of functionalism as a unity of ethics and aesthetics in a rational and architecturally sensitive engagement with technological challenges to design, building processes and societal planning.

In extension of this perspective, Chapter 4 describes how Vilhelm Lauritzen Architects manifests and realizes the modern project's ideals of community and enlightenment in educational and commercial architecture, in part by approaching the functionality and spatiality of architecture in a broader context.

In closing, Chapter 5 discusses how Vilhelm Lauritzen Architects has managed, from day one, to combine exquisite refinement with efficient functionality within a modern framework. The chapter also suggests which aspects of the modern project the firm will continue to develop.

Lunch break at Vilhelm Lauritzen Architects on the balcony in Nordhavn.

Since Vilhelm Lauritzen Architects has been part of this journey from the early beginnings of modern architecture, the firm's works and practice provide the story's main theme and perspective.

17

21

The modern project

Vilhelm Lauritzen Architects
and the modern utopia

Modern architecture is one among many artistic and societal expressions of the still fairly contemporary phenomenon known as 'modernity'.[3] The term applies to the era that began with industrialization, urbanization, the inclusion of science and technology into production and everyday life, secularization and autonomous, modern art. The German philosopher Jürgen Habermas called modernity 'an incomplete project'. The associations to architecture and planning in this statement are hardly coincidental. The modern project took on a characteristic ideological expression with the emergence of modern architecture and urban planning during the early decades of the 20th century. Taken, in a broader sense, to apply to civilization as a whole, this project, according to Habermas, dates back a hundred years before aesthetic or cultural modernity, to the Age of Enlightenment

The Stockholm Exhibition in 1930: functionalism arrives in Scandinavia. Long, horizontal modern lines, aerodynamic shapes, light and air, an expression reminiscent of an ocean liner. At the top of the building is Restaurant Paradiset (Paradise Restaurant). The horse-drawn carriage in the foreground was undoubtedly included to make a point: the future is already here; it is time for the past to move along.

and its expectation that 'the arts and sciences would promote not only the control of natural forces but also understanding of the world and of the self, moral progress, the justice of institutions and even the happiness of human beings'.[4] Modern phenomena such as international cooperation on peace and developmental aid, social safety nets, public health systems, science based on facts and empirical studies, a system of justice where everyone is equal before the law, freedom of speech and religion, independent mass media, a publicly funded education system and so forth all have their roots in this ideal and are part of the modern project.

Vilhelm Lauritzen Architects continues a firm that was founded just as modern architecture, under the enthusiastically waving banner of functionalism, emerged in Denmark and the other Nordic countries: 'The new shapes in architecture denoted a style of liberty, their social function was to express equality', to quote Gregor Paulsson, the creative mind behind the 1930 Stockholm Exhibition, which marked the breakthrough of Nordic functionalism.[5] However, a hundred years is a long time, and by now any obligation towards the ideals of early modern architecture might have long since evaporated in keeping with the tradition of new generations defining *their own* modernity and rejecting as antiquated anything that was once considered modern.

That would have been an understandable development. Surprisingly, however, that does not seem to have happened. Since 1922, Vilhelm Lauritzen Architects have improved human lives through functional architecture and design. The firm fearlessly declares in the first sentence of its 'manifesto'.[6] Here, the ideological term 'functionalism' has been translated into the more pragmatic term 'functional', and 'liberty' and 'equality' are replaced by the less grandiose and more contemporary term 'human lives'. However, being contemporary, and thus pragmatic and diplomatic, is quintessentially modern, and the point is clear: the modern project may be incomplete, but it has not been abandoned. And the contribution of architecture remains undiminished, even though it has, paradoxically, become harder for it to deliver the desired improvement of human lives, despite unprecedented prosperity and technological possibilities.

Thomas Scheel, architect and partner of Vilhelm Lauritzen Architects, says about the current conditions for his profession: 'Our society is profoundly shaped by the market economy, which is fine, in many ways. But of course, this means that economy rules. In construction, the only thing that isn't quantifiable is architecture. And it suffers because of that.'[7]

Architecture suffers because it has taken on the thankless task of preserving a utopia without which the modern project in a society that is 'profoundly shaped by the market economy' is often reduced to achieving the smallest quantifiable common denominator on the market: saving on everything to be able to afford more and more. The German modern architect Mies van der Rohe's oft-maligned slogan 'less is more'[8] – countered by the postmodernist retort 'less is a bore' – is really an acknowledgement that exquisite quality raises the quality overall. In that sense, the utopia, the unachievable, becomes a counter-image to the vast number of achieved objects that, after a short lifespan, end up as the environmentally disastrous, floating plastic island known as the Great Pacific Garbage Patch.

According to the prevailing instrumental version of rationality, only the quantifiable holds real value, and the non-quantifiable is banished to the realm of utopia. When modern architects consider the utopia of the good life an obvious architectural task, this is because the seemingly tangible qualities of architecture might in fact be just as elusive to rationalization as a hope, a dream or a yearning.

As another architect and partner of Vilhelm Lauritzen Architects, Anne Møller Sørensen, puts it: 'We can never stop imagining what doesn't yet exist.'[9]

This is exactly where the architect comes into the picture. In the modern utopia, we need to create the good life ourselves, rather than leaving it up to God, destiny or the conditions of social legacy and class. Life is a project – a building project, if you like, since the good life is shaped in the social community, which, precisely because it is not determined by God, destiny or conditions, must first be *built*. Thus, the modern project is fairly concrete, as utopias go, and consists to a high degree of the correlation of physical setting and mental well-being that we call architecture.

We might also call it a 'social experiment', parcelled out in the various areas of the larger plot of the good life. One such area is humanism, since human well-being is inextricably associated with the idea of being the centre of our own life and, on a larger scale, of humanity being the centre of all life. Thus, humanism is perhaps most essential in the realm of mental health.

A gigantic, humanistic experiment

Vilhelm Lauritzen Architects has taken on the core, humanistic aspect of the modern social experiment on several occasions. In a review in the professional journal *Arkitekten* of Vilhelm Lauritzen Architects and Karlsson Architects' psychiatric hospital in Slagelse (2015), Mike Rømer wrote that the project is 'the biggest of its kind in Denmark in recent years, but, more interestingly, it is also a gigantic experiment. Virtually all the solutions aim to create a healing architecture where traditional approaches and treatment forms are replaced by user involvement, transparency, joint ownership and a good dose of common sense. The underlying form and functions of the hospital have been thoroughly explored in an open dialogue between architects, staff, patients and relatives without a list of evidence-based answers or any ironclad guarantees that the various decision would actually work as intended. That is remarkable in a project of this scale, and, not surprisingly, the project has attracted a good deal of attention from abroad.'[10]

Experiments imply the risk of failure. And with high construction and operation costs, public architecture is subject to considerable political and media scrutiny. The fact that these projects are taxpayer-funded is a convenient point to bring up when other arguments fail. As is 'the changing times', an inescapable fact that no one can ever convincingly define. Politicians want re-election, and the media

Nature has a documented healing effect on people. In combination with the low, densely spaced buildings with warm brick walls, the small courtyard gardens provide a calm, reflective space for psychiatric patients.

want stories, so everyone involved in major building projects come equipped with lawyers and advisors who offer a host of instruments for addressing the unquantifiable: descriptions of services, risk analyses, process management, stakeholder analyses, exemptions of liability or user satisfaction surveys. Self-inflicted problems such as budget overruns, delays, corruption, dismissals of those responsible and so forth almost seem to be part and parcel of construction projects, although they are probably much-publicized exceptions. What is in fact an inherent aspect, however, is the ever tighter process management and the excessive planning and architectural caution that the fear of these scandals has caused.

Thus, it takes courage and stubbornness to engage in a 'gigantic experiment' without the reassurance of 'a list of evidence-based answers'. With the psychiatric hospital, the architects sought to put some of the most vulnerable members of society, patients with mental illness, in the role of building clients.

What might they want if they were not primarily seen as the object of treatment? This question undoubtedly echoed the staff's desire to deliver dignified treatment to those who, most of all, present a risk to themselves. In itself, the implied question – what does a dignified setting look like? – aptly illustrates how far the architect's task is from rational risk analyses. Indeed, Rømer wrote that the architects tellingly 'had a hotel in mind'. Although treatment usually lasts longer than the average hotel stay, it is not hard to see what they were aiming for with that mindset: a place permeated by the everyday non-treatment life of non-patients.

What might they want if they were not primarily seen as the object of treatment?

A spa hotel for the mind

In keeping with this notion, the patient section looks nothing like a hospital and more like a development of cluster houses. Inspired by Arabic architecture, in Denmark this type is particularly popular as senior housing. It is also represented in beautiful, peaceful, classical and highly sought-after housing developments such as Jørn Utzon's Fredensborg houses. The patients' rooms face green courtyards, turning the outdoor greenery into a natural extension of the interior. In his review of the hospital architecture, Karsten Ifversen, the architecture critic at the Danish newspaper *Politiken*, noted how some of the first Danish psychiatric hospitals – Risskov, Sct. Hans and Oringe – were designed to resemble manor houses with spacious parks, 'because it was assumed that expansive greenspaces would have a calming effect on the patients. However, a walk in the park can be literally overwhelming to an ailing mind'. Hence, in Slagelse, 'the park moved inside'.[11]

From the patient rooms, a large section of the interior wall can be opened to the circulation space to enable contact with the social life unfolding around the patient and people passing through the corridors. 'Thus, the individual patient can choose how to engage in everyday life, and if it all becomes too much, the large doors can quickly be shut to restore privacy. That is a thoughtful solution', Mike Rømer added, and he is right.

That freedom of choice evokes some of the best qualities of the high-density, low-rise collective housing or assisted-living facilities. It offers the safe feeling of a flat or single-family house but without the isolation inside tower blocks or behind hedges that most people face, and which is probably itself an important source of disorders.

Throughout, the thoughtful and carefully planned spatial interpretation of an important need in both patients and staff reflects empathy and dedication. Rather than the anonymity of a hotel, it is the homeliness of the private sphere that characterizes this semi-public institutional setting – but, importantly, with the touch of luxury that a good hotel offers. After all, few people have their own private pool, not to mention an 'intimate water environment, where the individual patient can relax in a safe, sheltered setting – almost like the wellness section of a modern spa hotel', as noted by the critic in *Arkitekten*. The hospital's open but flexible office landscapes with meeting rooms, lounge areas and a wide range of facilities for physical activity or relaxation reminded him of modern corporate HQs. A spectacular curvy veneer-lined stairway, its shape accentuated by lighting, adds to a sense of exclusivity that we normally associate with official meeting and reception rooms. Only, here it is not intended to impress investors, shareholders and business associates from abroad but designed to promote recovery. Another characteristic is a talented interplay of art and function in the decoration of the many glass dividing walls with quotations from poetry as well as a stimulating colour scheme throughout the complex, matched to the hand-moulded bricks in the facade cladding and the muted natural colours of the courtyard gardens.

The Fredensborg houses (1963) by Jørn Utzon. Perhaps one of the world's most convincing alternatives to both the single-family house and the block of flats.

The psychiatric hospital in Slagelse is the largest psychiatric facility constructed in Denmark for the past hundred years. The hospital has 650 employees and 194 beds.

The norm – an experiment we can put behind us

Modern spa hotel, exclusive corporate HQ and a successful experiment with a hand-moulded approach in more than one sense. The human mind is poorly suited for evidence-based answer sheets. As striking as this is in a design intended for psychiatric patients, it is also a reminder for us all.

Or, as Karsten Ifversen wrote: 'The patients are met with respect, as equals, and their illness, which prevents them from enjoying their freedom, should not deprive them of the pleasure of quality spatial settings. Humanism has become a cliché in the discussion of Nordic architecture, but here it is on full display. Everything is designed to support the individual patient's unique treatment. The goal is always for the patient to return to the community as a normally functioning member. A psychiatric patient is someone who needs help to achieve independent self-reliance.'

The project in Slagelse suggests that sometimes the experiment ought to be the norm, and what is considered the norm is an experiment we can put behind us.

Architects face the fundamental dilemma of the modern project: on the one hand, rationality and efficiency are crucial for a functioning welfare society. On the other hand, the point of this social structure is that it accommodates its less efficient members and aspects – people as well as details, however quirky they might be.

Rather than hiding behind the norm, however, in this case, the architects insist on taking a chance on humanism, which has allegedly 'become a cliché' because the big expectations it raises have so often ended in disappointment. Empty promises leave the words bereft of meaning.

In disappointment over the encounter with, for example, the treatment environment of a technocratic and bureaucratic health system, the humanism of the modern enlightenment project is perceived as the opposite: as patronizing and dehumanizing. Angry over the broken promise of mutual humanity, we yell at those who think they know better and who, in fact, often do but who are trapped in the objectifying role of the treatment professional vis-à-vis the treatment object: the patient. On the other hand, the person-turned-patient also often slips into a predefined role, adopting psychologizing language and accepting treatment and the role as patient in a negative cycle where the act of turning one's own body and mind primarily into an object of treatment ultimately becomes self-fulfilling.

Vilhelm Lauritzen Architects' design of the psychiatric hospital in Slagelse was created for some of the people who are now often, characteristically, described as society's 'most vulnerable' members. No walls offer shelter from the storms of the mind. So what can architecture do for this group? The first step is to insist on humanism rather than research-based evidence. The next is to strive for genuine innovation. In a dialogue with the people involved, the architects need to challenge the traditional hierarchy between staff, patients and relatives. Shred the conventional view of hospitals as inherently different from hotels and corporate HQs – or homes, for that matter. And finally, cut through all the handed-down notions of the asylum and its monastic asceticism and dare to design for the good life. Bearing in mind what this means for the most vulnerable in our society.

The architecture integrates spaces, flow and building components in a way that promotes recovery through the interplay of light, shadow, materiality and colour, among other features.

'Humanism has become a cliché in the discussion of Nordic architecture, but here it is on full display. Everything is designed to support the individual patient's unique treatment.'

Humanistic functionalism

Part of the reason why the humanistic perspective is now considered a cliché is that in our ingrained Western individualism, we may find it hard to imagine a human being not being free. Our notion of freedom is individualistic, and an individual seems a very specific and well-defined entity: ourselves. From that perspective, the slave's or the feudal tenant farmer's involuntary acceptance of the state of affairs or the deeply devout believer's voluntary decision to relinquish their freedom to the divinity and the religious community appears equally hard to fathom. From an individualistic point of view, humanism is the presumed condition – naturally, I am the centre of my own world.

To the humanists in the city states of Renaissance Italy, however, individual freedom was not given but a concept that held the seeds of rebellion against the powers of the church, the state and the arts.[12] Ever since, authoritarians of every ilk have been suspicious of the humanities, not to mention the humanistic perception of justice that underlies the concept of human rights.

The rejection of the irrational power of authorities is one of the two main pillars of humanism. The other is Enlightenment's confidence in knowledge as a rational power factor. The rationalists of the Enlightenment found that scientific results and technology offered more reliable guidelines for human edification and the design and development of society than the tolerance, common sense and good judgement of the Renaissance humanists. Indeed, it was in the new construction methods, mass production and liberated aesthetics of technology that the modern architects in the early 20th century saw a connection with the social aspect of architecture. That connection was called functionalism.

One of the young Vilhelm Lauritzen's earliest projects after his graduation as an architect from the Royal Danish Academy of Fine Arts in Copenhagen was for the architecture competition 'Urban plan for the port town of Hanstholm' (1923). Lauritzen did not win, but his project received an honourable mention along with other projects, and in the architecture journal *Architekten* [sic] his colleague Steen Eiler Rasmussen highlighted Lauritzen's entry as nothing short of exemplary.[13] The key lesson to be learnt from Vilhelm Lauritzen's project was that neither strict geometric dogma nor other formalistic excesses of style make sense; what is called for is careful groundwork, including a thorough analysis of conditions and needs. That will enable an urban plan that 'corresponds to the town's functions', as Rasmussen wrote in his commentary.

Here, functionalism is neither an ideology nor a style, and even though it might be both in many manifestations of modern architecture, it is worth noting that to a modern architect such as Vilhelm Lauritzen, the modern liberation from stylistic constraints was always bound by an obligation to ensure that the design worked, both in aesthetic and pragmatic terms. Unlike many of the other participants in the competition (many of them engineers, by the way, since at the time urban planning was still considered mainly a matter of road construction), Lauritzen did not believe that traditional, grandiose Parisian-style boulevards, 'star-shaped squares and axes' were right for the small town of Hanstholm on the North Sea coast. In his project, the streets hug the terrain, sensitive to both nature and navigability. The distribution of functions considers wind conditions and the mitigation of unpleasant smells from industry and the port.

For industry he proposes that a 'location [...] north and north-east of the town will be the least bothersome in terms of smoke and unpleasant smells, as wind from these corners is rare, the north wind blowing 4.3 per cent of the days of the year, the north-easter 9.3 per cent'.

Research and precision pay off. Especially if one wants to prevent economics and aesthetics from being positioned as competing concerns in the assessment of the project:

'The terrain that becomes the town centre is the flattest and thus the most economical for the construction of the costliest streets. The line shaves the top off the hill where the lighthouse stands. The hill is shaped as a flat dome, on which the houses would be beautifully clustered, with increasing building heights towards the top. From outside, the roofs will appear one above the other, echoing the dome shape of the hill, only with a slightly steeper slope.'[14]

The main street in Lauritzen's urban plan is not a straight line but forms an arc between the port and the railway; this avoids unnecessary gaps and oblique angles and allows for expansions to accommodate future growth. His plan even includes modern considerations of interactions:

'It would be unfortunate if the town were further divided by the establishment of a third isolated district around the railway, both for the cityscape and for the communication between the districts. [...] [To] spare the partially cultivated area around Hanstedmølle Huse, it is proposed to turn it into a plantation, which could accommodate sports grounds and similar elements and might play a role in local activities as a venue for political meetings, popinjay festivals and similar events.'[15]

Vilhelm Lauritzen ensures the cohesion of the new town and its connection with the existing fishing hamlet by designing a dense, urban structure combined with areas set aside for nature, recreation and future expansions. This functionalist approach ensures the necessary connectedness or cohesion, or as Steen Eiler Rasmussen mused in his comment on the competition, it is good to have a city that functions and 'unfortunate when a large, regular star-shaped square lies empty and abandoned. [...] In art, no shapes, no details have value in themselves, they only derive value in context'.[16] As art historian Lisbet Balslev Jørgensen concludes in the book on Vilhelm Lauritzen: 'Lauritzen's architecture was created for man's needs at each time'.[17]

The man-made Kronløb Island in Copenhagen's Nordhavn district is Denmark's 432nd island. It contains housing and a car-free urban space that is only accessible via three footbridges. Rendering from the competition proposal.

Modern and postmodern nature

Vilhelm Lauritzen Architects did not design the urban plan for Copenhagen's new Nordhavn district, but the firm has created many buildings in the area, and more are on the way. Most of them are

Unlike many of the other urban spaces in inner Nordhavn, Kronløb Island has a lush, diverse green landscape with native and carefully selected other plants – a contrast to the surrounding canals.

The foundation of Kronløb Island contains an underground car park below the water level. The photo shows the construction of the man-made island in 2020.

housing, and one of the more spectacular examples is the Kronløb Island project (2023), which was designed in collaboration with another Danish architecture firm, Cobe, on Kronløbsøen, which has been presented as 'Denmark's new island'.[18] It is a man-made island in the Kronløbsøen basin, which was established in 1918 as an expansion of Frihavnen (the Free Port) and named after Kronløbet, the water north of Trekroner island, which connects Copenhagen Port with the Kongedybet fairway.

Denmark is continuously gaining new islands as a gift from the forces of nature in the form of sea currents and erosion. Over the past 30 years alone, nature has thrown up at least 138 new sand banks. Most remain uninhabited, occupied only by birds, which thus gain badly needed new breeding grounds. Man-made islands are rarer and are mostly created in connection with bridge construction. Currently, there are also plans for the construction of large man-made islands dedicated to offshore wind farms in the Baltic and North Seas, although they are likely to be off limits to the public.

This 9,000-square-metre island, on the other hand, is very much inhabited, with both a bridge and a tunnel link. At the narrowest point, the island is only 15 metres from the mainland, so there is no reason for the new residents to feel isolated. The building has a total floor space of 25,000 square metres, distributed over six floors, with 233 flats and a small number of shops and other commercial spaces. The island is car-free above ground but features a three-storey underground car park with room for 1,100 cars. This is probably a good deal more than the residents will need, and, indeed, Vilhelm Lauritzen Architects expects that the 'underground car park will be the entrance to Nordhavn for many motorists'. To architecture enthusiasts, the staggered tiers of balconies, plateaus and incisions in the light-coloured stone that is reflected in the water around the island might bring to mind one of the most famous buildings of modern architecture, Frank Lloyd Wright's Fallingwater from 1935.

In addition to the attraction of waterfront living and, for some residents, the sweeping views of the port and the Øresund strait, the building is, not least, interesting because it attempts to 'imitate nature', as the project landscape architect STED puts it.[19] Not only are the many 'random' displacements in the exterior walls designed to evoke the image of Danish cliffs, such as Møns Klint; the large inner courtyard was envisioned as a 'green mountain valley', with 'lush plantings'. That is no easy task on this site, and the landscape architects carefully sought out plants that are hardy enough to handle salt spray from the water and to thrive on top of a deep underground car park. These plants come from what might be called Denmark's 'primordial forest', the 'pioneer species' that are the first to set down roots in a place and prove hardy enough to survive. Still, the vision requires the use of special light-weight 'super soil' and 'advanced irrigation systems'.[20]

Naturally, it would be easier simply not to build on a man-made island in the middle of a port, as the project engineers readily acknowledge.[21] The requirements for the durability of the foundations are staggering, since there is no easy way to repair the foundations of an island. Tackling great depths of water and extreme water pressure, both from below and from the sides, the project has adopted a belt-and-braces approach. The building is dimensioned to stand up to worst-case scenarios and events, including storm surges, the crush of ice and even a ship collision. 'A wayward ship cannot be allowed to cause the island to crack', as engineer Kåre Flindt Jørgensen from the contractor NCC points out.[22]

Naturally, the decision to turn a windswept pier into a rocky landscape with greenery sprouting out of every crack is driven by the desire to create the best of all worlds, the urban woodland, nature on our doorstep, without the inconvenience of having to live in nature, far from urban amenities. Kronholm's architectural expression supports this imitation of nature, with the randomly fluctuating play of greys in the facade cladding, the varying heights and divisions of the long, horizontal window bands and the striking play of light and shade created by the many displacements and reliefs in the exterior walls. This underscores the modernity of the architecture, in the sense that what matters is the spatial experience, not representation or, for that matter, the ability to blend in with the nearby architecture or the setting.

This makes it an overwhelmingly modern, autonomous, freestanding structure that insists on being a building *volume*, not a stage prop, like an elaborate baroque facade or a postmodernist 'decorated shed'. Instead, it is a stylized geometric version of a cliff or a mountainside or perhaps an active deconstruction of a less sprawling, classic modernistic building volume.

This exploration of depth, both in the depth of form and in the scientific depth of the geological and botanical concept, also applies to the sustainability of the complex, which is certified at the highest level because it takes every aspect into account, from the life cycle of the building materials, the transportation, durability and accessibility to the indoor climate and water consumption, both during construction and in use.

Just as architects often talk about 'giving something back' to the city, neighbourhood or street in their design and organization of a building, this may be seen as an attempt to give something back to nature in ecological and humanistic terms. Such an approach to the possibilities and conditions of modern, urban life and our complicated relationship with nature in a residential design could be seen as architecture's contribution to research areas such as human ecology and environmental sociology.

However, this intended natural architecture has another interesting aspect that is characteristic of our time, which is the effort to move beyond the inherent conflict between culture and nature in modern civilization and create a third element: a new or modern form of nature, shaped not by human utilization or exploitation but by our need to rediscover ourselves in nature. This effort includes the notion of a 'memory landscape':[23] a place that reminds us of another, recollected place. This recollected landscape is more elusive than the actual site, but through the suggestive power of recollection it takes on an intensity that surpasses reality and elevates a humble site to a stunning experience.[24]

What we might call 'modern' nature is profoundly shaped by cultivation and our attempts at making it inhabitable. While this has led to countless local environmental disasters and, by now, global climate change, which poses a direct threat to our civilization, it might be an apt reflection of our postmodern state that man-made nature on a man-made island is not perceived to present a paradox, let alone a conflict. Here, architecture imitates nature in the acknowledgement that we cannot replace it.

Architecture on a wilderness survival trip in America's dramatic nature: Frank Lloyd Wright's Fallingwater (1939) on the Bear Run river in Pennsylvania.

A machine for living in and the future of environmental technology

In 1923, the same year that Vilhelm Lauritzen designed his urban plan for Hanstholm, the Swiss architect Le Corbusier published an architectural manifesto that was immediately – and remains – recognized as the bible of functionalism. 'A house is a machine for living in. [...] An armchair is a machine for sitting in', he wrote in *Vers une architecture*.[25] During the early years after the First World War, modern architecture was so new that it could be described, as Le Corbusier aptly did, as something we were on the way 'towards'. In his self-confident view, he probably felt that humanity was now for the first time moving towards any sort of architecture at all.

The machine is used here as a metaphor for modernity itself: man-made, technological solutions to achieve the mastery of nature that is the basis of civilization. Machines are, by definition, functionalist, as their function is their sole purpose. That is why their 'nondescript' aesthetic was so popular in early modernity, not least in design and architecture. The notion of houses as efficient machines might have been intended as provocation, but it was not so far-fetched at a time when the dual goal was to break free from the arbitrary dictates of architectural styles and to improve the miserable housing standards that most people endured a hundred years ago.

Function has always been a key condition of architecture, as exemplified by one of the earliest known theories of architecture, the Roman architect Marcus Vitruvius Pollio's treatise *De architectura* from the late 1st century BCE, which was carefully studied by Renaissance humanists. According to Vitruvius, a building should possess three characteristics: *firmitas*, *utilitas* and *venustas* – strength, utility and beauty. Both during the Renaissance and from the mid 18th century to the present day, classicists have marked their allegiance to this preferred stylistic brand by symbolically including the distinctive elements of harmony, the orders of columns and so forth. In the modern project, that sort of thing is considered reactionary and irrational.

During the earliest times of the modern project, in the Age of Enlightenment, the French architects Étienne-Louis Boullée and Claude-Nicolas Ledoux sought to reduce architectural expression to basic, geometric shapes as a way of capturing the inherent 'nature' of shapes, things and ideas. Architecture historian Emil Kaufmann argued that Ledoux 'wanted to reflect the intention of the time by pure architectural means' and saw a straight line from Ledoux to Le Corbusier. This line also marked the distinction between modern and obsolete, rational and traditional and pulled architecture free from academic painting and sculpture and thus the history of style through consistent abstractions until the expression arrived at the building's pure mass and space.[26] A century later, when industrial construction techniques made it possible to achieve this liberating abstraction, the modern project thus already had an ideological superstructure, rooted in the Enlightenment, which turned the combination of rational form and function into 'functionalism'.

Machines are, by definition, functionalist, as their function is their sole purpose. That is why their 'nondescript' aesthetic was so popular in early modernity, not least in design and architecture.

A modern wooden building

From 1947, Vilhelm Lauritzen was the first chairman of the board for the Danish Building Research Institute, an important role for ensuring the contribution of architecture to the modern project in Denmark. One key task was to find efficient methods for addressing the huge housing shortage after the war. Another was to industrialize construction without compromising on quality while testing new methods and materials. This engagement reflects Lauritzen's interest in science and technology in general and the development of the architectural profession in particular. Vilhelm Lauritzen Architects' continued commitment to these topics is reflected in the firm's use of cutting-edge digital tools and its engagement in the development of future environmental technology by testing new construction systems.

This includes the design of Denmark's tallest building to date with timber as its load-bearing construction. The frame of the six-storey building on Østerbrogade 190 in Copenhagen is not made of steel and concrete but of timber and concrete. The construction utilizes a new modular system developed by the Austrian company Cree based on prefab elements in a hybrid material consisting of concrete and cross-laminated timber.

From outside, the building looks like a modern boxy construction with a window grid, but inside the timber is exposed in order to reveal the structure, in the spirit of functionalism, and to imbue the interior with the warm, organic, 'Nordic' qualities of the wood. Above the ground floor, intended for a café or similar function, the building has five storeys with a total of 20 small student dwellings. The flats are cross-lit through floor-to-ceiling windows offering the young residents a view of city life.

Every aspect of this wooden high-rise is modern: its avant-garde use of innovative sustainable materials and construction methods, its fairly new architectural target group, the way it not only exposes but makes a virtue of its construction, its deliberately contextual design, and its conception and design as modern architecture as reflected in its spatial organization and aesthetic expression.

Like many other areas of future technology, architecture's role in leading civilization away from its course of self-destruction and ecological depletion will surely reproduce nature's own solutions in many ways. Perhaps the functionalist machine for living in is not as artificial an idea as it might seem. Machines can be many different things, and machines, computers or robots that successfully imitate human nature are expected to have a bright future. Not because they replace human beings but because they imitate our nature and capabilities.

Fascination with pure geometric shapes in the lead-up to modernity. The French 'revolution architect' Claude-Nicolas Ledoux's unrealized project Maison des Gardes Agricoles (Rural Guardians' House) from 1770.

41

Houses for people

Crisis and social reforms

In Denmark, we refer to our local version of modern civilization as the 'welfare state' or the 'welfare society'. Naturally, like the modern project, this society has been underway for a long time.[27] The claim that the Danish welfare society is more or less the same age as Vilhelm Lauritzen Architects is based on the Danish political reaction to the global economic crisis from the late 1920s into the early 1930s. This crisis led to political reforms which added a social dimension to Danish society matching the spread of democracy. This *social* dimension became the core of the social democratic or social liberal welfare society, which also exists in the other Nordic countries and which is probably the most crucial Scandinavian invention.

The crisis made it clear that the rapid modernization of society, along with industrialization and urbanization, meant an end to naturally determined and

Krøyers Plads (2016) in Copenhagen. Through dialogue and inclusion, Vilhelm Lauritzen Architects managed to gain the approval of the local residents and transform the site from an urban battleground to an award-winning urban space.

43

A new phenomenon was brought into the world: urbanization, with cities claiming new land and country people turning into city dwellers. With distances shrinking, the perception of time and space became modernized.

traditional conditions and ways of life and brought in not just conveniences such as electric light, indoor plumbing and motor vehicles but also alienation and slums. Unless the state provided what has become known as a social safety net, market forces would make the poor even poorer and incapable of driving the demand needed to keep the selfsame forces going. By pointing out the downsides to the market economy and the importance of public investments, Keynesianism – named after the British economist John Maynard Keynes, who formulated it – had a decisive impact on the fiscal, labour and social policies of the welfare state.

Industrialized manufacturing of standardized products generated jobs and also kept the cost of these products so low that ordinary people could buy them. Take Henry Ford, who repeatedly lowered the price of the Ford T while raising pay for his workers. Not as an act of charity but because it was good business: it enabled his workers to buy the cars they were making; soon Ford's company was the biggest in the world.

However, industrial production and market forces did not seem to be capable of eradicating poverty and inequality alone. As a result of poverty and rapid urbanization and industrialization, most people continued to face miserable living conditions well into the modern era.[28] Even today, in some of the biggest cities in the West and in developing countries, living conditions in large slums resulting from intense urbanization continue to trap the poorest people in a hopeless situation.

Thus, in order to understand why architecture came to play such a key role in the construction of the welfare society, it might be worthwhile revisiting the history of urbanization.

Urbanization and the campaign for better housing

During the 18th and 19th centuries, Europe's rural population grew, as more efficient methods of cultivation and, thus, greater crops meant that a smaller workforce could feed more people. The resulting surplus of labour in the country caused many people to migrate to the cities. In Denmark, however, industrialization got off to a late start; some have argued it did not really happen until the mid 20th century. In the mid 19th century, most Danes still lived in the country, and even if life here might be in tune with nature, as the Romantics would put it, it was also tough, in a constant struggle for survival, especially for smallholders and day labourers with little or no land. This will have made industrial jobs seem alluring: imagine getting paid for one's work!

In terms of the physical environment, in just a few decades, industrialization caused explosive growth in cities, which had only expanded very slowly over the past 500 years. A new phenomenon was brought into the world: urbanization, with cities claiming new land and country people turning into city dwellers. With distances shrinking, the perception of time and space became modernized. Time was no longer marked by the first arrival of the lark or the blooming of the heather but by the factory whistle and the train schedule.

Housing shortage

The growing focus on residential architecture during the early 20th century reflected a *professional* interest in connecting with vernacular architecture and national traditions in a time of upheaval and change. However, it was also driven by a new *social* engagement in the living conditions of ordinary people with particular focus on the growing housing shortage.

The urban housing shortage had persisted since the late 19th century; in Denmark, it was particularly pronounced in Copenhagen.[29] The problem applied to all the cities of the industrialized world, and the housing issue was on the political agenda throughout Western Europe, including in the young Danish democracy. Like progressive politicians, architects began to listen to the physicians involved in the sanitary movement, who in newspaper articles and lectures drew attention to the public health impact of the ruthless overcrowding in overbuilt, old, often medieval, city centres,[30] where sanitation well into the 20th century meant an outdoor privy in the courtyard to be emptied after dark by the 'nightman'. In Denmark, new legislation in 1933 required that all inhabitants in Copenhagen have access to a water closet – on the floor of their dwelling.[31]

Up until the city ramparts were opened in 1852, and the no-man's land just beyond them turned into new built-up neighbourhoods, virtually no residential rental properties had been built in Copenhagen, apart from extensions into the courtyards, so demand was huge. Even after construction began, it could not keep up, and enterprising builders took advantage of the rudimentary regulations to create high-density multistorey buildings. Typically, the poorest and largest working-class families had to make do with tiny, overcrowded flats with poor sanitary conditions in densely built-up courtyards without access to fresh air or daylight. Meanwhile, speculative construction in the poorly regulated market meant that many flats stood vacant, because workers could not afford the rent in superior buildings.

The well-meaning reformers in the English garden city movement and the architects of the Bauhaus school[32] were right: modernity was an architectural issue, and architecture needed a social profile – for example in the form of urban planning and 'social' housing.[33]

Following spread: Pier 2150 (2020) in Copenhagen's Nordhavn district provides all the flats with daylight and access to outdoor spaces and a shared intimate courtyard in the centre.

45

Dronningegården (1942) by Kay Fisker, C. F. Møller and Svenn Eske Kristensen. One of the most accomplished results of the clearances of Copenhagen's miserable jerry-built housing from the late 19th century.

The housing complex Fortkaj (2021) in Copenhagen's Nordhavn district is a reinterpretation of 1930s modernism and the classic rectangular perimeter block inspired by Kay Fisker.

Brickwork and density

Skipping ahead for a moment to contemporary residential architecture in Copenhagen's recently urbanized Nordhavn district, it soon becomes clear that the combination of national architectural traditions and a social, humanistic perspective has given Danish modern architecture a distinct unified character.

In both expression and function, Vilhelm Lauritzen Architects and Cobe's residential complex Fortkaj (2021) in Nordhavn draws on the best aspects of Danish neoclassicism, which marked the transition to the particular national interpretation of architectural modernism. The red bricks, laid in long, horizontal relief bands with red joints, the red window frames accentuated by white window niches and the delicate red railings clearly, as the architects point out, draw on inspiration from the Danish architect Kay Fisker, who more than anyone personifies the thinking behind 'gentle' Danish modernism and also created some of the finest residential architecture of his time. In a time of housing shortages, Fisker's large housing blocks Hornbækhus (1922), Vestersøhus (1938) and Dronningegården (1943) were perfectly economical, both in terms of construction costs and the sparse neoclassicist expression of the uniform but well-proportioned long facades.

Fortkaj is a loyal interpretation of this model but also departs from it, fortunately, since the 200-metre-long facade and vast interior courtyard of Hornbækhus is structurally out of step with our current expectations of urban housing. Varying the building heights, facade rhythms and textures, along with the more intimate courtyards featuring raised vegetable beds and, for example, the tall window sections and raised-up balconies of the ground floor, lends the traditional, five-storey red housing block a lighter, more elegant and more welcoming appearance. One key advantage of brick is that it ages beautifully, and Fortkaj's simple, recognizable features serve as an independent extension of the Østerbro district's successful recipe for good housing. Moreover, it has an experiential and spatial density and an absence of cars that would undoubtedly be welcome in many places in Østerbro.

Although decent dwellings have become affordable to more people since the 1930s, the modern project's vision of the capacity of architecture to enhance society remains limited by the structural constraints on construction, whether in the form of building regulations or market forces. However, Fortkaj demonstrates that by simple means and with a sense of refining the most successful elements of the genre, it is possible to achieve considerable renewal and improvement, even within fairly narrow limitations.

A similar observation applies to Vilhelm Lauritzen Architects' Pier 2150 (2020) in the new dense neighbourhood among the former warehouses in Nordhavn. A key source of inspiration for the Nordhavn development was the attractive atmospheric Dutch neighbourhoods, sheltered among canals and warehouses, often highly accomplished and widely admired by architects. In stark contrast to the Ørestad district, the converted warehouses serving as design showrooms, offices and studios provide a very different and essential street life. Pier 2150 consists of 68 dwellings. Although they are owner-occupied flats, the balconies and patios and the short distance between the buildings give them many of the same qualities as a co-housing development.

Concrete slum replaced old slum with a brutality that made many prefer the old version. As a material, concrete developed a reputation as grim, unswervingly bureaucratic, insensitive, inhumane and bleakly modern.

Despite the distinguished expression of the facade with grey bricks, dark grey window frames, elegantly rounded modernistic balcony corners and long, horizontal but ample window bands, the development resembles an adult-scale doll's house, lively and with rich opportunity for contact and communication in and out of doors and windows, up and down stairs and in between exterior niches and windbreaks. As the name reveals, this is waterfront living with low steps and ledges towards the water, and with proper supervision (this is, after, all, a port), Pier 2150 must be a much better place to be a child – and a young family – than the heavy housing blocks of the 1930s, with their large courtyards and unsafe streets.

Kanslergade Agreement

In the 1930s, however, construction took place in the shadow of a housing crisis that, unlike today, was embedded in a larger economic crisis. Back then, the Depression drove unemployment above 30 per cent, and events in the large neighbouring country of Germany showed the possible ramifications of this crisis.

However, the same day as Hitler came to power in Germany, there was a crucial development in the Danish housing sector. On that day, 30 January 1933, Prime Minister Thorvald Stauning's Social Democratic Party and its Social Liberal coalition partner reached the 'Kanslergade Agreement'[34] with the historically rural Liberal Party. In Danish history, this agreement is seen as emblematic of the strength of Danish parliamentary democracy and the ability of people to settle disagreements through pragmatic compromise while, just south of the Danish border, extremism was leading to disaster. Above all, the agreement represents a milestone in the establishment of the Danish welfare state. In addition to meeting the Liberal Party's demand for a devaluation of the Danish krone to promote agricultural exports, the partners agreed to simplify social legislation and generally replace the humiliating principle of alms with an entitlement to social assistance. And, not least, the housing initiative: in order to solve two of the most urgent problems of the time, unemployment and the housing shortage, the partners decided to boost public works and offer incentives for construction. Housing, and thus architecture, became an independent policy area. The main instruments were state loans and dedicated loan schemes, especially for social housing. That set things in motion, and by the late 1930s there was actually a surplus of housing.

Concrete and crane tracks

To the progressive modern architects of the interwar years, the metaphor 'machine for living in' still had an optimistic ring. As they saw it, mass production and its promise of making the good life possible for the majority would naturally also include the fundamental need for decent housing.

In fact, housing was such a common building type that, apart from palaces and mansions, until the modern era it was not generally considered an architectural discipline. Architecture was considered an art form and, as such, the reserve of the wealthy upper class. Architecture had to do with representative buildings, palaces, churches and elegant homes. Ordinary people built their own houses with assistance from local builders. The architectural style was vernacular, handed down and largely determined by locally available materials and skills.

Today, a 'machine for living in' has a different ring, not least because industrial construction, which made it possible to meet the housing need, also laid bare all the inhumane aspects of modern, economic rationalism. Concrete slum replaced old slum with a brutality that made many prefer the old version. As a material, concrete developed a reputation as grim, unswervingly bureaucratic, insensitive, inhumane and bleakly modern.

While the rational industrial approach was largely an optional stylistic expression in early modern architecture during the interwar years, it became the prevailing dictate of housing construction after the Second World War. Material shortages brought construction to a virtual standstill during the war, especially private projects, but people kept migrating to the cities. Thus, after the war, the housing shortage was back on the welfare agenda.

Both in the reconstruction of Europe's war-torn cities and in the Five-Year Plans of the Soviet Union, rational, industrial prefab high-rises were seen as the solution. 'Crane track construction', where the distribution of housing blocks was determined by the track width of the construction cranes, was cheap and, above all, fast. In large developments, with mass-produced standard elements and a limited degree of variation, the overall impression was bleak and ugly compared to architecture's traditional attention to detail and individual expression. The order and harmony that modern architecture had inherited from classicism as well as its own functionality, material authenticity and pared-down simplicity suddenly appeared meagre and poor. When the residents then added the bourgeois interior style they had been raised with, the droopy frilly curtains in the cheap standard windows only added to the bleakness.

Based on the concepts of humanism and housing as a machine for living in, contemporary urban planning aimed for a functionally divided city with high-efficiency industrial areas separated from quiet, green, recreational residential areas. To those who could afford it, the alternative to a prefab flat in a high-rise was a prefab standardized detached house, designed to fit into the garden cities or bedroom communities in the urban zone plan. That required extensive new traffic infrastructure for commuters, and since the social democratic policy was based on Keynesianism, which saw public investments in, especially, infrastructure as a way to generate jobs and improve the economy, adding public transport and motorways to the welfare package was an obvious move.

The flats had all mod cons and offered vastly improved housing standards for the poorest residents, but the post-war 'crane track construction' lacked all other qualities, not least a human touch, and gave concrete a bad name.

Concrete blocks and standardized detached houses spread throughout the country at an unprecedented rate. From 1950 to 1980, one and a half million such homes were built, corresponding to an average rate of 136 every single day, including Christmas. Thus, in the modern era, architecture would become a mass phenomenon.

Concrete construction solved the specific problem of giving people a roof over their heads, but it also gave the modern project, including its architecture, a decidedly bad reputation and resulted in widespread suspicion of urban and societal planning. Laypeople felt that if the responsible architects persisted in and even defended their work, it must be architects *per se* who were the problem. For their part, architects often felt marginalized in building processes where budgets were so tight that the architect's professional latitude was reduced to a standardized lowest common denominator. Architecture historian Nils-Ole Lund summarizes this unfortunate state of affairs from an architect's point of view:

'Construction became more and more contractor-controlled and production-oriented, and although the technical standard rose, the home became more a commodity than an architectural product. When at the same time the single-family house market moved from the architects to the tract house manufacturers, a large part of housing construction disappeared from the "architectural sphere".'[35]

Still today, the challenge of creating a machine for living in seems to be too tall an order for our societal construction.

People in and between the houses

Since the turn of the millennium, the cost of both owner-occupied and co-op housing has been steeply increasing, in part because favourable loan schemes have made property investments more attractive. However, if few people can afford to live in the city centre, the buildings here end up as office space for advertising agencies or law firms or as pied-à-terre for wealthy Danes living abroad. That creates a whole host of problems for urban planners and politicians. Hence, affordable housing is a recurring political topic in many cities, including Copenhagen.

One of the core principles for Vilhelm Lauritzen Architects is that good architecture is for everyone, and that everyone is entitled to quality housing, regardless of their social status and income. Hence, on several occasions, the firm has entered into collaborations to develop and construct affordable quality housing.

In a framework agreement with the social housing association Lejerbo, Vilhelm Lauritzen Architects is currently building 1,500 small, affordable dwellings for the Startbo project. The concept is based on providing affordable homes conceived in a straightforward expression with a distinctive architectural and material character.

The Bella Rows (2017) in Ørestad is a development of 122 terraced houses with a simple expression built in robust materials. It incorporates inspiration from 19th-century dense Copenhagen neighbourhoods, such as Kartoffelrækkerne (1889) and the later Humleby development (1891), based on a vision of forming a communal social setting around small houses.

The dwellings combine modernist functionality and clearcut forms with precisely composed variations and a vivacity that the stricter variants of modern architecture sometimes lack.

A Danish rendition of typical English terraced houses: the aptly named Humleby (Hops Town) near the Carlsberg brewery in Valby, designed by Frederik Bøttger for Arbejdernes Byggeforening (Workers' Building Association).

Thus, both the material selection and the principles guiding the detailing are simple, and the construction principle is highly industrialized and largely based on prefab elements. Still, by combining different exterior materials, it is possible to give each area its own character.

In several residential projects, Vilhelm Lauritzen Architects has thus sought to combine tight budgets and efficient land use with the preservation of high quality throughout based on thoughtful design, usefulness, durability, high-standard materials and on-site plans and layouts that encourage social interaction among the residents. The dwellings combine modernist functionality and clear-cut forms with precisely composed variations and a vivacity that the stricter variants of modern architecture sometimes lack.

Bellarækkerne (the Bella Rows) (2017) is a development of 122 terraced houses in Ørestad on the edge of the green common Amager Fælled, near Bella Center. The demand for efficient land use is met by the construction of three-storey buildings. Thus, despite offering a floor space of up to 124 square metres, each house has a footprint of just 45 square metres. The materials are brick in muted earth tones, slightly varied to ensure that the development as a whole has a coherent but not completely uniform appearance, and wood which fades to light grey. The exterior expression is similarly slightly varied with asymmetrically positioned elements, producing a composition that is dynamic without being busy.

The compact houses have a kinship with well-known Copenhagen building association houses, such as Kartoffelrækkerne (the Potato Rows) and Humleby (Hops Town), and their close contact and organization around narrow lanes and small squares with plants, sandboxes, benches and so forth enhance 'the life between the houses', to quote the Danish architect and urban planner Jan Gehl's famous phrase. Each house has a front and back garden, but these private spaces are merely a discreet marker and a transition to the semi-public space of the development overall, sheltered from full public view. Contact with the neighbours is facilitated, at once open and non-committal; residents can be visible and secure, present without participating or fully engaged in the life that is unfolding around them.

This carefully balanced cadence in the expansion of the dwelling's private space is almost impossible to achieve in the spaces around the many Le Corbusier-inspired, modernist concrete blocks of the post-war era. Tall, solitary and exposed to the elements, they are too far from the ground, and even though the flats are close together, the residents are far apart, since the buildings uniformly prioritize views, air and light and in practice – counter to intentions – favour privacy and individualism. Each family gets its own 'drawer' in the high-rise, and from the balconies everyone faces the same way: away from each other.

Reinterpreting the modern legacy

In 1943, Vilhelm Lauritzen designed the site plan for the Høje Gladsaxe development, which was constructed in 1966.[36] With their prominent presence in the landscape, the five tallest buildings, 16 storeys high, demonstrate the monumental power of modern architectural expression and offer testimony to the efficiency of industrialized building. The development, which took just three years to build, offers nearly 2,000 affordable dwellings, hypermodern for their time and totalling 40,000 square metres. In addition to the dwellings, the project features large green spaces, a municipal primary and lower secondary school, preschools, shopping centres, a library and a church – in short, a fully functioning town.

Compared to the Bella Rows, it is obvious that the modern legacy had to be reinterpreted to ensure that variation, warmth, traditional materials, such as bricks, and life between the houses are prioritized ahead of clear-cut shapes, efficient concrete and expansive open space. It is simply a matter of salvaging the modern project's intention of giving society a social profile and turning physical environments into a setting for the good life that promotes the common good – rather more than a setting, in fact, when one considers how important housing is to welfare, well-being and our sense of belonging.

Another example of Vilhelm Lauritzen Architects' engagement in the housing agenda of the modern project by taking advantage of industrial prefab elements in order to keep the costs down without compromising on quality is the development of the building concept CLT Flex.[37] The firm sends 3D models of the building components to a company that produces them as solid elements in cross-laminated larch wood ready to be assembled on site. Simple, cheap and fast. The flexibility of the system makes it possible to construct many different housing types, from small one-room flats to large units spanning over two and a half floors with ample space for families. The system can also be used to construct, cluster and vary structures both within the individual buildings and among them to create interesting spaces, passages, recreational areas and transitions between indoors and out.

The first project using this building system was completed in 2019. It is located in Skademosen, near Trekroner, and appears a far cry from what one might expect from low-cost, industrialized prefab construction, as one recalls the crane track approach. The impression is rather that of a small cosy town, consisting of two-storey houses loosely distributed in a meadow with tall grass, almost reminiscent of the familiar, naturally aged Swedish village: common areas, garden spaces and patios with gentle transitions and an informal, welcoming air throughout. The exterior cladding is the building system's standard untreated greying larch with patches of roofing felt and a discreet band of solar cells on an asymmetrical pitched roof. The facade of the top floor slightly corbels out past the lower floor, window heights and sizes vary, and the small bicycle and waste-bin sheds have the same expression, like offspring of the houses, forming spaces and adding a little shade and privacy.

The overall impression is of a place that is intimate, safe but also rational and smart. High-density low-rise cool, perhaps. A mindset and a design that arose in response to modernism and which has now, apparently, returned.

Skademosen (2019) consists of 44 two- to three-storey residential timber buildings just outside Roskilde. The buildings are placed in two horseshoe-shaped garden spaces, with six long blocks in one and seven in the other.

The timber buildings in
Skademosen are built using
an extremely climate-friendly
construction system. The
buildings are programmed
as 3D models, which are then
produced as solid cross-
laminated timber elements to
be assembled on site.

Social mindset and environmental awareness

There is no single answer to how architecture can turn social and physical environments into a setting for the good life that promotes the common good. This is in part because the context that early modern architecture and, especially, the international style tended to treat as uniform is now an essential and highly variegated basis for design and planning. That variation can promote the common good might in fact be a fairly advanced and late modern insight.

However, the acknowledgement in recent years of the need to reinterpret the legacy of modern architecture is not just due to the negative experiences from crane track construction. It also stems from a general 'expansion of consciousness' in the welfare society, as the social mindset of the labour movement from the first half of the 20th century was picked up a couple of decades after the war by the generation of the youth rebellion in 1968, who combined this social mindset with a new environmental awareness.

The latter was a response to a phenomenon brought on by industrialization and the welfare society: pollution. The traditional agricultural society was largely an ecological circuit, where the only added factor was hard labour. Industrial production is a different matter entirely, and over the course of the 20th century, the combination of private enterprise and the lack of knowledge and public regulation proved, literally, a toxic cocktail.

When the chemical plant Grindstedværket moved the most polluting elements of its production from Grindsted in western Jutland to Grenå in eastern Jutland on the Kattegat coast in 1970, the openly stated reason was that the powerful northbound sea current off the Fornæs point would carry all the toxic stuff far away – out of sight, out of mind. Grenå City Council agreed and welcomed the new workplaces.

The 1960s also saw the emergence of a critical consumer movement, not least in the United States, where the consumer advocate Ralph Nader – who later ran as the Green candidate for President – took on the automotive industry for ignoring car safety. This critical stance grew into a broader environmental awareness, which eventually spread to the political level. Thus, Denmark appointed its first minister for the environment in 1971.

Alternative housing forms, alternative ways of living, alternative mindset. In the 1960s, young people were rebelling, rejecting conventions and turning the hierarchy of needs on its head: what do we actually need?

Squatting democracy

The 1968 student rebellion illustrated that the modern project produces its own harshest critics. The youth took the intentions of the project seriously and did not see how the utopia of the good life for the common good could be achieved by the middle-class suburban lifestyle, which was also increasingly being embraced by the working class. They were critical of the authorities and politicians of their parents' generation, who might have succeeded in rebuilding society after the war but who were now content with having a modern flat or a detached house and a wider selection at the local supermarket. In their complacency, the critics argued, they had forgotten what really mattered: that the motor of the project is continuous enlightenment and a critical mindset. The youth criticized the prevailing lifestyle and culture and pointed out that the democratic project was far from fully accomplished. For example, they argued, it had yet to spread to the workplace, where men still decided that they should be paid more than women, or to the universities, where the professors decided the curriculum.

The concept of environment promoted by the environmental movement was quite broad, ranging from working conditions and pollution to urban planning. Thus, environmental awareness came to drive a new wave of the growing social outlook of architecture that the housing issue and functionalism had initiated before the war. This was evident in particular in the actions of the squatters, who during the 1960s and 1970s protested the extensive clearances of old, unhealthy housing developments, for example in the Copenhagen districts that had been built after the ramparts were opened. Slum clearances were mainly driven by the pursuit of the modern sanitary principles of light, air and hygiene from around 1900 and involved the wholesale demolition of entire neighbourhoods to be replaced with new buildings. With few variations, this policy was shaping urban planning in all Western European cities at this time. However, to the young squatters and many others, this was not an environmental improvement. Even if they saw the point of building new housing with modern conveniences, many lamented the damage to the local environment. Also, the planners typically did not bother to ask people what they wanted but simply assumed that the technocrats and bureaucrats knew best. Thus the chorus of a contemporary Danish hit song, 'Hands off our neighbourhood'.

Obsolete housing blocks ripe for condemnation and disused workshops and industrial facilities abandoned in the transition to a service economy had turned into slums and were being taken over by young squatters. Here, Sofiegården in Copenhagen in 1967.

Alternative needs

Resistance to modern urban planning and modern housing architecture revealed a serious flaw in the modern project: its failure to consider that the people it was planning and building for might not be quite as modern as society in general. They did not feel at home in modernity. Perhaps, this was not surprising, given the rapid and profound changes society had undergone in less than a hundred years.

The young generation of architects and urban planners argued that the project had to be rethought, and so it was. The reaction to the use of concrete was not only critical but also constructive – and 'alternative', to use the term applied, for example, to renewable energy forms, which have now become the norm and a necessity, with wind farms, electric cars and solar panels. Driven by social and envir-

The old unsentimental modernist Steen Eiler Rasmussen even defended the district as 'living, sprouting life, a green plant among the cobblestones. No law could build that, but the law could crush it. Do not let that happen!'

onmental awareness, people established communes and co-housing on undeveloped land. In diametrical contrast to the tower blocks of modern architecture, these were typically high-density low-rise developments, adapted to the site and its history. That seems to have been the right medicine for the project. The principles of light, air and community-building were preserved, and in recent years, the movement has even managed, to some extent, to bring these principles back to the city with thoughtful restorations of former industrial facilities, the use of recycled building materials and consideration for the life between the houses. Thus, rooftop patios, urban villages, urban gardens, urban ecology, round houses, communal spaces, conversation staircases, rooftop ski slopes, computer-generated 'wild' organic shapes and so forth are now changing the face of our cities. All of it, importantly, initiated only after asking the users what they want. The same trend applies to other consumer areas, where private companies preceded the public sector in the introduction of 'basic democracy' in the form of focus groups, product testing, satisfaction surveys, likes and so on.

The Danish poet Thøger Olesen tapped into the popular feeling with annoying accuracy when he wrote the lyrics for the 'Hands off our neighbourhood' song from 1970, criticizing the instrumental rationality of modern architecture and planning: 'No, it's not exactly modern / but it's everything we need.'

That was the crux of the matter. The modern project is meaningless if it fails to meet people's needs. Then the past becomes the 'good old days', even if we know this is just sentimental claptrap. Eventually, the squatters of the 1960s received the official stamp of approval of their actions to squat old buildings until they were due for demolition; they even had a specific section in the law, the so-called squatter's rule.[38] The 'free town' of Christiania, which had become the outpost of self-governing alternativism, survived every change in political majority in Copenhagen's City Council and even, more recently, an architecture competition. The old unsentimental modernist Steen Eiler Rasmussen even defended the district as 'living, sprouting life, a green plant among the cobblestones. No law could build that, but the law could crush it. Do not let that happen!'[39]

Since that time, architecture and urban planning have been under the scrutiny of a critical and environmentally and socially conscious public. Welfare architecture was politicized from the outset and still seems an area where free market forces might clash with public interest. The fact that profit-hungry equity funds, such as Blackstone, continue to be able to buy up properties, to the despair of local politicians and residents, offends our sense of fairness. The power of environmental awareness is that it encapsulates the essence of the welfare society: the good life for the common good. Most people realize this vision in a life revolving around family, home and work – ideally in a harmonious triad, right where they are.

Architecture as a political flashpoint

These developments have made architecture a political flashpoint, as Vilhelm Lauritzen Architects has experienced on several occasions. In Krøyers Plads (Krøyer's Square) in Copenhagen, the firm put its head in the mouth of the critical public.

Krøyers Plads is located in Copenhagen's Christianshavn district, and, like Nordhavn, it was freed up when the industrial port activities were discontinued or relocated. Above all, though, it was a hot potato when the owner of the site, NCC Property Development, asked Vilhelm Lauritzen Architects to develop a project proposal in 2010.

A few years earlier, a furious public had rejected the winning project in an architecture competition, the Dutch architect Erick van Egeraat's project of six high-rises, one of them 14 storeys tall. Objections were voiced by the Academy Council of the Royal Academy of Fine Arts, by Foreningen til Hovedstadens Forskønnelse (the Society for the Embellishment of the Capital) and by the European cultural heritage organization Europa Nostra, which had Prince Henrik as its president. In addition, more than 14,000 citizens, a record number, signed a petition objecting to the project in 'our beloved Christianshavn'.[40] 'There are never going to be high-rises on Krøyers Plads', as one newspaper headline concluded.[41] In fact, many argued there should be no buildings at all on the site. The City Council got cold feet and turned the project down.

Community sketching

To build on Krøyers Plads, the architects would need to stage a design process that involved not just the client, the authorities and the future residents of the buildings but also, and equally importantly, the general public in and beyond Christianshavn. As Thomas Scheel of Vilhelm Lauritzen Architects put it, the architects' process had to focus on 'putting aside our company ego. We had to be *the architect*, rather than Vilhelm Lauritzen Architects'.[42] The form had to accommodate not just function but also *process*.

To achieve this, Vilhelm Lauritzen Architects, NCC, Copenhagen's City Architect and GHB Landscape Architects engaged the local community in a process of basic or participatory democracy. Specifically, the firm held three themed workshops where everyone could debate the project with the architects and the client and contribute ideas and requests. The client insisted on being completely honest with the public: NCC would listen to the locals but never hid the fact that the project had to be economically viable, so whatever happened, something would be built. 'To our surprise, the local resistance was not really about the building plans as such. People

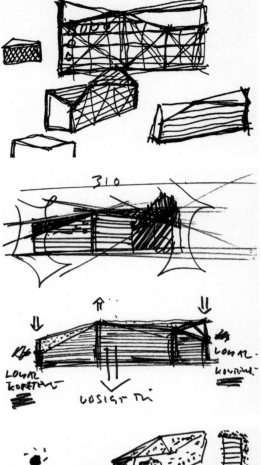

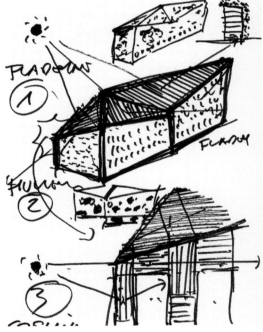

In the early stages of the development of Krøyers Plads, Vilhelm Lauritzen Architects facilitated three workshops with the local residents. The participants' input was subsequently converted into preliminary sketches, where many of the ideas from the workshops were clearly incorporated into the architecture, including the placement of the three individual buildings, the open lines of sight to the water and the variations in height that created the characteristic geometric roofs.

The three buildings on Krøyers Plads contain 105 dwellings and a ground-floor café. The fractured crystalline surfaces of the roofs and facades create variation in an expression that otherwise loyally blends into this historically sensitive warehouse environment.

simply had strong feelings about what it should look like and wanted someone to listen', Thomas Scheel explains.

Summaries from the workshops, which took place in spring 2011, are in the public domain, and they make interesting reading.[43] The bone of contention in this sort of conflict between architecture professionals and local residents is almost always the same: the professionals want to create 'visionary' architecture, often in the form of tall, monumental buildings, while laypeople want something 'green' and low, with a village feel. The lay perspective is often a mix of fairly pragmatic self-interest and, as mentioned earlier, a deep-seated environmentally conscious critique of civilization that has a long history in modernity as a critique of progress and its negative consequences. Hence, paradoxically, so-called alternative attitudes often appear quite conservative.

The workshop summaries from the Krøyers Plads project confirm this trend but also show that if environmentally conscious, enlightened, modern citizens are given a voice, they often prove to possess no small amount of knowledge about the elements of architecture and urban planning. This knowledge is based on an intuitive, genuine and autonomous understanding of how the physical environment can promote the good life. This is where the layperson's autonomous, modern environmental consciousness meets the autonomous, modern architect's professional pride. Thus, at a tangible, local level, there is a good chance that the utopia of the modern project can be realized, unless commercial or bureaucratic interests get in the way. As they often do.

Based on that experience, many professionals have adopted a rather cynical view of reality. Thus, Karsten Ifversen cautioned that this expanded democracy was unlikely to result in qualified contributions: 'This type of community involvement goes well beyond traditional public hearings. It is a type of urban development that uses participatory democracy to build local goodwill, but it also risks leading to disappointment, since some ideas will not be feasible.'[44]

Nevertheless, the community dialogue resulted in a new detail plan proposal, which enjoyed support from all the stakeholders. Many of the characteristic qualities found at Krøyers Plads today can be traced back to the community input, including the angled roofs, the height, the open lines of sight and the placement in relation to the historical warehouses. In 2011, Vilhelm Lauritzen Architects and GHB Landscape Architects established a partnership with Cobe to design the site in accordance with the new detail plan.

Based on that experience, many professionals have adopted a rather cynical view of reality. Thus, Karsten Ifversen cautioned that this expanded democracy was unlikely to result in qualified contributions.

The juncture of Strandgade and Krøyers Plads is highlighted with a kink in the building; the new tactile bricks offer a respectful counterpoint to the historical yellow-brick warehouse. Krøyers Plads is an exceptional example of the incorporation of new buildings into a historical urban space.

In one of the three buildings the architects turned the bricks on edge, adding a tactile quality and a subtle relief structure to the brick wall.

Turning the brick and building a new site

Vilhelm Lauritzen Architects and Cobe's[45] housing development at Krøyers Plads consists of three buildings forming a loose, staggered block around the dock. The building volumes and roofs are angled and truncated with a rich use of skylights and balconies in order to maximize harbour views and the influx of daylight. The construction is concrete, but apart from a long exterior wall in black anodized aluminium, the exterior is clad with custom-made extra-wide hung tiles with a pronounced tilt, which produces a relief mosaic and creates a sense of weight and kinship with the solid walls of the old warehouses along the waterfront, even though the brickwork is not load-bearing.

That this is a modern interpretation of the historical harbour front environment is subtly suggested by the fact that the bricks are turned around, exposing the 'frog' – the interior cavity designed to hold extra mortar. Thomas Scheel explains:

'It is a fairly simple but by no means arbitrary feature. We chose brick, because it matches the environment here at Holmen, as a material that is used in many of the historical buildings. On the other hand, architects also need to have the courage to depart from history and make new choices. To build houses with character.'[46]

The roof construction represents a similarly bold, vitalizing modern interpretation. Considering the dominant role of the roof in the expression of a building, it is surprising how overlooked it seems to be in architecture. The pitched roof sits heavy on the average Danish house, and many a roof is a major detractor from the appearance of a landscape. It is only in the past twenty years that roof design has begun to gain momentum, especially in cities and in spectacular projects where public space continues onto the roof, transforming into anything from a picnic site to a ski slope.

On Krøyers Plads, the deconstruction of the familiar pitched roof into flapping butterfly wings makes a striking effect. Prismatic shapes are trending in contemporary architecture, but here, in combination with the variation in the brick cladding, it does not come across as faddish or contrived but as a variation on the traditional pitched roof and the general building style in the area, with its heavy structural volumes and other, later buildings in a similarly compact style. A similar quality is found in the studio's conversion of a former smithy in Aarhusgade in Nordhavn, Frikvarteret (2015), where a jagged shed roof forms a new top floor, referencing the site's industrial history, and adds a distinctive new aspect to the facade – an aspect that interprets the context while adding new functions, such as rooftop patios and windows.

On Krøyers Plads, the roof design adds interior floor space and makes for more interesting rooms. That is important, as the 38 flats, which do not have a residence requirement, are very high-end properties; in fact, one of them had the highest ever asking price for a Danish flat. They feature wide Pomeranian pinewood floorboards and custom-designed kitchens, and according to the Danish newspaper *BT*, NCC called this part of Christianshavn 'the Hellerup of Copenhagen', referring to the posh beachfront area north of the city.

The most priceless quality is perhaps that Krøyers Plads seems to have become a successful new locale in Copenhagen, offering all Copenhageners access to the harbour front. Through the

combination of form and process, the project has found a relevant answer to the functional requirements. It is no easy task to combine contextual responsibility with originality, especially when strong forces tug at the architect's arm every time he or she sits down at the drawing table. Such are the terms in the modern city, where people live and shape their opinions and identities in the close interactions of the public square. Construction automatically becomes urban planning and thus a public affair, albeit on the terms of the market economy and private enterprise. That is an explosive cocktail, as demonstrated by the Krøyers Plads project, but in this case the story appears to have a happy ending, because the stakeholders were able to work together and turn the brick inside out.

The functionalist legacy

It is interesting to see how the public sphere, with its dual aspects of public debate and public space, is capable of providing the interactive setting that is often the condition of creativity. With Krøyers Plads, it was far from obvious how architecture could match the functions in accordance with the intrinsic purpose of the modern, functionalist legacy. Although we should assume that the public sphere and the approach to architecture in public space has changed quite a bit from early modernism to now, it seems clear that Vilhelm Lauritzen Architects has, more or less deliberately, preserved Lauritzen's mindset and approach, even though he never asked the tenants or residents but stuck to measurements and careful reflection.

However, some of the challenges that early functionalist modern architecture, in its liberation from tradition, tackled with great precision still seem relevant, perhaps even timeless, to the architecture firm. Among the examples of the legacy that Vilhelm Lauritzen Architects manages is a number of similarly thoughtful and strikingly timeless public projects from 1930s and 1940s Danish welfare architecture designed by Lauritzen.

In 1936, Vilhelm Lauritzen won an architecture competition for a new town hall for Gladsaxe, a suburban municipality near Copenhagen. Like so many other progressive European cities during the interwar years, this growing municipality modelled its urban development on the German city Frankfurt am Main. During the Weimar Republic in the 1920s, architect and urban planner Ernst May had overseen the development of Das Neue Frankfurt (The New Frankfurt), new districts complete with housing, schools, sport facilities and many communal green areas with playgrounds and so forth. Frankfurt's urban development under May was further characterized by high-quality architecture produced on a fairly modest budget with a pioneering use of simple prefab elements. Among other sites, his Römerstadt remains a place of pilgrimage for architecture students to this day.

Römerstadt (1928) in
Frankfurt am Main by Ernst
May – the English garden city
successfully translated into
German Bauhaus style.

Top: Gladsaxe Rådhus –
stage one, 1937.

Bottom: Gladsaxe Rådhus –
stage two, 1953.

Lauritzen's Gladsaxe Town Hall (1937/1953) consists of two sections and two construction phases. It was originally designed as two mirrored L-shaped wings, combined to form a stylized human figure with its arms outspread, with the council hall to be placed in the 'torso' as the 'heart' of the finished town hall building. During the second construction stage, in 1953, this plan was altered, and the extension was designed as a block with a slightly pulled-back top floor. The modern but also reverential architect considered it 'a reasonable requirement of a town hall that the facade has a quality appearance and ages with dignity' and concluded that the most affordable material to meet these requirements was red brick.[47] Lauritzen personally designed the interior with an exquisite sense of light, rhythm and consistency in the placement of wall lamps and the design of the pleasantly rounded push plates on the elm-wood doors echoing the slight dome shape of the lamps. A recent (2012) refurbishment of the town hall, intended to make room for more employees by establishing open office landscapes while also improving the indoor climate and acoustics and installing newer and more climate-friendly energy optimization, was recognized with Realdania's Renover (Renovate) award for 'gentle renovation'.

After the success with the town hall, Lauritzen acted as an urban planning consultant for Gladsaxe until the mid 1940s and also designed a sports centre, a library (Søborg Library, 1939) and three schools, Marielyst Skole (1938), an expansion of Bagsværd Skole (1939) and Stengård Skole (1952).[48]

These building projects share a similar expression, constructed in reinforced concrete faced with red brickwork and furnished almost exclusively with designs from Lauritzen and his studio. They appear as holistic and appealing designs with beautiful detailing and excellent durability both aesthetically and in terms of the choice of materials and solutions. They are exemplars of functionalism, stripped of superficial mannerisms. The single-storey Stengård Skole with its carefully staggered, intersecting building volumes is both a functional learning environment and welcoming to the pupils, especially the younger children, who might feel lost and overwhelmed by the scale of a big school. With its low buildings and pitched roofs, it also blends into the suburban neighbourhood: 'An intersection broke down the classical concept of space and gave greater freedom in planning. [...] There were no expensive, noisy staircases, the walls were thinner, and all ordinary classrooms could be given access to both the garden and the corridor', as Lisbet Balslev Jørgensen comments.[49]

The key point that continues to underpin functionalism to this day is that functional qualities should not be considered as separate from constructive or aesthetic ones. All three aspects are affected by how daylight is pulled into a corridor: a lobby serves as both an assembly hall and an arrival space; a stairway forms such a beautiful space that it is more than just a passage on the way to somewhere else; and facade cladding leaves the corners free – all examples from Lauritzen's buildings in Gladsaxe, which appear timeless in their carefully considered detailing.

Renewal in context

In Copenhagen's Vesterbro district, the combination of politicized housing construction and community-driven urban planning returned Vilhelm Lauritzen Architects' proposal back to sender until the architects realized they needed to design an 'infill': filling out the gap in a row of buildings.

The building in question is located on the corner of Istedgade and Viktoriagade, and if one did not know better, one would think it was as old as its neighbours and not from 1999. But appearances are doubly deceiving here, as this is in fact a fully authentic brick-built structure, not the usual concrete construction with thin brick facing designed to reconcile a skimpy budget with the locals' (and most Social Democratic mayors') affinity for traditional Danish brickwork.

In this case, the architects had decided to prove that a brick-built structure 'can more or less hold its own against the sandwich elements of industrialized construction',[50] as the professional journal *Tegl* wrote with poorly hidden glee, even though the critic was clearly facing a tough dilemma: On the one hand, this was an 'anachronism, [...] the building virtually blending in with its surroundings'. On the other hand, the journal, which was published by the Bricklayers' Association's Information Council, could hardly put down a brand new, multistorey brick building constructed in the age of concrete. Besides, this was clearly quality architecture.

Tegl found that 'in accordance with local traditions, many fine features have been introduced to add some small degree of architectural character. By discreet means, the building stands out slightly from the adjacent buildings, which undeniably contributes to the unity and variation of the streetscape. The building has smoothly finished recesses, and the widest of the piers appear in fair faced brickwork in the full height of the building. These sections feature mortar in a range of colours to match the cadence of the rhythm from house to house in the street'.

In addition, the solid craftsmanship meant the building would have 'many years ahead of it – with very little maintenance'. It also offered good dwellings, despite the limited space offering 'an airy spacious sense [...] and with diffusion-open exterior walls and plastered brick walls everywhere inside – there are no gypsum walls – the indoor climate undoubtedly offers good conditions for a healthy environment with effective air change. The building already has the stamp of approval from the Danish Asthma and Allergy Association, which has first claim with the Lejerbo housing association to some of the flats'.

The Vesterbro corner building was part of an experiment launched by Realdania, the urban renewal firm SBS Byfornyelse and the Bricklayers' Association's Information Council. The experiment set out to determine what it would take to give brick buildings a role in construction again. Was it too costly? Too time-consuming? Do the bricklayers still have the requisite skills? Will the difference in quality be noticeable? The experiment provided new insights, including, in this case, the perhaps unexpected finding that good buildings do not always match the criteria for their assessment. Suspending for a moment the knee-jerk reaction of 'where are the visionary qualities?' this is simply a good building that people could enjoy. If that is not welfare architecture, what is?

With its low, staggered volumes, Stengård Skole in Gladsaxe (1952) adapts to the surrounding suburban neighbourhood. The school was constructed during a time of material shortages and thus favours local materials such as brick and timber.

Good architecture and anachronism. This building on the corner of Istedgade and Viktoriagade in Copenhagen is so well adapted to its environment that at first glance it resembles the neighbouring 19th-century buildings. However, the simple lines and crisp detailing of the facade show the modernist influence. The building is from 1999.

Suspending for a moment the knee-jerk reaction of 'where are the visionary qualities?' this is simply a good building that people could enjoy. If that is not welfare archi-tecture, what is?

The concept of the strong solitary building that modern architecture inherited from classicism is still considered architecture's most autonomous artistic achievement. However, architects are not sculptors, and architecture is not a liberal art form. Thankfully. The utilitarian requirement is one of the key qualities of architecture, and if it has its abstract artistic qualities, its expression is still a wonderfully concrete setting for life.

The premises for the Vesterbro project did include certain cautiously worded principles for urban renewal (no longer referred to as 'slum clearance'), informed by the traumatic experiences from the turmoil sparked by urban renewal in the neighbouring Nørrebro district. However, that is part and parcel of the highly politicized area of housing architecture. In a sense, the atmosphere in an area is an equally important part of the context as the brickwork of historical warehouses. Vilhelm Lauritzen Architects had successfully completed a challenging infill task and could take pride in noting that their brick-built structure was 'realistically competitive on time and cost in comparison to industrialized construction'.[51]

Challenging the design of clinical rationality

The term 'welfare' implies that society is well on the way but has yet to reach its goal. 'Prosperity', on the other hand, has a ring of static contentment, perhaps even complacency. With an unprecedented level of societal and personal prosperity, and with the housing issue more or less resolved, welfare architecture has in recent years focused increasingly on healthcare, an area of growing concern to an ageing, well-situated and well-fed population, where people have a roof over their head (in some cases, several roofs). In recent years, the Covid pandemic has put health and disease at the top of the global agenda, from its impact on individual everyday life to the global circulation of goods, communication and travel – or, rather, lack of it.

Health architecture is also an important category in Vilhelm Lauritzen Architects' portfolio, especially if this is expanded to include life-sciences education architecture, an area in which the firm is developing growing expertise. That makes good sense. The humanities, social issues, engineering and life sciences are key focus areas in the rationale underlying the modern project. On the other hand, there can be a certain uncanny quality to the modern healthcare system; although its mission is to protect us from life-threatening disease, it can also feel like a technocratic contraption. That is why 'clinical' has such a negative ring to anyone outside the medical field. Indeed, modern architecture has consistently been criticized for having a chilling laboratory aesthetic. On a yacht, the white surfaces and stainless steel may be admired as the essence of functionalism, associated with speed and high living, but in the clinic they remind

An icon of modern architecture: Alvar Aalto's tuberculosis sanatorium (1933) in Paimio, Finland.

The vision driving the New North Zealand Hospital (scheduled for completion in 2025) is that there is more to life than just being alive. Here, the architecture seeks to break down the boundaries between illness and health. Drawing on new knowledge about healing architecture as well as classic concepts of scale, spatiality, materiality and nature, it aims to promote well-being for patients and visiting relatives.

The architecture was conceived as a living organism where the landscape becomes an ecological part of the building, which engages in varied and adaptive communication with its surroundings and itself. Despite a total floor space of no less than 118,000 square metres, the New North Zealand Hospital maintains a human scale, most of it just two storeys high.

us of the sharp edge of the scalpel, our wretched body stretched out, helplessly, under a sterile sheet.

This makes it an important architectural task to make the rational institutional 'health space' liveable and humane. After designing Finland's national pavilion for the World Exposition in Paris in 1937, the Finnish architect Alvar Aalto commented:

'One of the most difficult architectural problems is the shaping of the building's surroundings to the human scale. In modern architecture where the rationality of the structural frame and the building masses threaten to dominate, there is often an architectural vacuum in the left-over portions of the site. It would be good if, instead of filling up this vacuum with decorative gardens, the organic movement of people could be incorporated in the shaping of the site in order to create an intimate relationship between Man and Architecture.'[52]

Aalto went on to do just that with his superb tuberculosis sanatorium in Paimio (1933), a consistently modern design with white exterior walls, large surfaces, rounded balcony corners and long horizontal window bands. Surrounded by tall pine trees, it is the essence of a modern sanatorium, but it is far from clinically bleak.

Similarly, the New North Zealand Hospital, designed by Vilhelm Lauritzen Architects and the Swiss firm Herzog & de Meuron (scheduled for completion in 2025), may be a so-called super hospital – and it is very big indeed: no less than 118,000 square metres – however, as the project description puts it, it is designed 'on a human scale [in] harmony with the surrounding landscape'.[53] The building's shape, resembling an amoeba or a flower, organically winds its way through the landscape like a plant, looking more like a museum of modern art than a scientific-technical institution. With curves, varying garden and landscape spaces and extensive use of light-coloured timber, both in the exterior walls and inside, the architects clearly sought to break up the strict monotony of concrete, steel and glass characterizing traditional large-scale institutional architecture with its long, straight corridors and arbitrary, left-over outdoor spaces. However, it also considers the crucial factor for design durability, which is that buildings that see heavy use have to do more than simply stand up to wear and tear and actually become more beautiful with time and use. Naturally, only time will tell whether the building will in fact achieve the beautiful patina that characterized the solid quality materials of older architecture, but the laudable ambition is that the building will 'over time appear as a patinated, Nordic furniture classic – tactile and showing the traces of the people who used it before you',[54] to quote the project description.

With a similar ambition, Vilhelm Lauritzen Architects, working with Mikkelsen Arkitekter, designed a facility for Steno Diabetes Center Copenhagen (2021) next to Herlev Hospital. Due to the emphasis on economic rationality and efficiency, institutional architecture, including hospitals, is often so big that what architects call 'scale' – the proportional ratio between person and building – seems alienating and distancing. In settings that deal with issues of vulnerability, disease and death, where the need to feel safe and secure is greatest, architecture often lets us down. Under the heading of 'homeliness and community', Vilhelm Lauritzen Architects thus goes so far as to describe Steno Diabetes Center Copenhagen as 'a house where you feel at home'. This is the very opposite of the experience we often associate with institutions such as hospitals, where we might, at best, feel that we are in safe hands but which are definitely not a place anyone would want to call home. Or, as the architecture

Japanese finesse combined with an intimate, Nordic welcoming atmosphere. The green gardens are a central element of Steno Diabetes Center Copenhagen (2021) in Herlev.

firm puts it: 'For people with diabetes, it is crucial that Steno Diabetes Center Copenhagen is a place where they do not feel stigmatized as being "sick" – a feeling that a cold and alienating treatment environment can often convey. Steno Diabetes Center Copenhagen is a warm and welcoming house that offers a safe, homely setting.'[55]

The first thing the architects did to turn something that obviously is not a private home into 'a house where you *feel* at home' was to change the ratio between the human scale and the scale of the building. Unlike the economically rational utilization of the building site that a high-rise offers – and in stark contrast to the neighbouring Herlev Hospital, Denmark's tallest building, at 25 storeys – the Steno Center is not much taller than a detached single-family house.

Both storeys are constructed around green atriums with tall trees, since, as the architects put it, 'being in nature is vitalizing'.[56] There, exterior walls have a lot of glass, but since the nearest surroundings are designed as a natural landscape, the impression from certain angles is almost like that of a nature resort. That feeling is enhanced by the widespread use of wood, both as flooring and as battens on the interior facades in the atriums, in ceilings and as stair railings.

The long lines and deliberate minimalism of a design approach focused on statics and geometry draw on the heritage from early modern architecture. In contrast to its confident swagger and authoritative planning, however, Vilhelm Lauritzen Architects refers to a design strategy 'that is not based on any absolute architectural form but instead an adaptive concept'[57] with 'multi-purpose spaces'.

Of course it could be argued that the architects had little choice, since that is the kind of strategy that wins healthcare architecture competitions these days. Budgets will vary, new treatment methods will be added, structural changes in the healthcare system will lead to mergers and closures, and in just a few years, the priorities the architects seek to accommodate in the building programme may have radically changed. The paradox prevails: flexible architecture endures.

There is no doubt that Vilhelm Lauritzen Architects considers the absence of what they call 'spectacular absolute form' as a strength that makes room for 'an architecture where variation in spatial scale, influx of light, materiality and contact with nature set the tone', and that it is no shame to acknowledge, as they do here, 'the understated character of the architecture'.[58]

On the contrary, as demonstrated by the residential buildings on Krøyers Plads and the psychiatric hospital in Slagelse, there are good reasons for architects not to insist on a strong and dominant pre-conceived design but instead to listen, reflect and identify with the users and to try to convince the client of the benefits of a project that is going to 'pay off' over time. Perhaps measured on parameters or instruments that are not as immediately obvious as the scalpel or the pocket calculator but which are crucial for the ability of architecture to help achieve the good intentions of the wider modern project.

Studies show that traditional hospital environments can make even healthy patients feel less capable and even ill. Meanwhile, other studies have found that spending time in green environments makes people more likely to report good health. Based on this knowledge, Steno Diabetes Center Copenhagen is designed with outdoor areas that encourage physical activity and an interior that promotes healing and learning.

Following spread: This bird's-eye view shows the organization of Steno Diabetes Center Copenhagen around a green space on two levels with small verdant gardens and a public roof garden.

1922–1999

1922	Daell's Department Store
1937	Gladsaxe Town Hall
1945	The Radio House
1956	The People's House, now VEGA
1964	TV-Byen
1998	Terminal 3

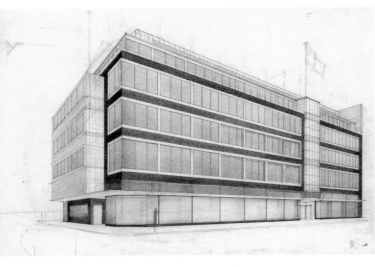

In 1922, Vilhelm Lauritzen and Frits Schlegel won the first competition for Daell's Department Store, which became a household name during the 20th century. The department store was known especially for its mail-order catalogue, which in the 1970s was sent to almost every second Danish household. The building was completed in 1924, but a few years later the Daell brothers initiated its expansion to a new department store. Meanwhile, modernism had arrived, and both brothers liked this new architecture. This time, Lauritzen merely designed a modern, simple facade with long window ribbons. The facades were plastered in a colour shade matching the Church of Our Lady, with the pillars concealed under white paint to make the long window ribbons appear uninterrupted. The left image shows Vilhelm Lauritzen's sketches for the refurbishment of the department store on Nørregade in Copenhagen (1930).

Daell's Department Store, 1922 and 1935, Copenhagen,
in collaboration with Frits Schlegel in 1922, after 1922
Lauritzen on his own

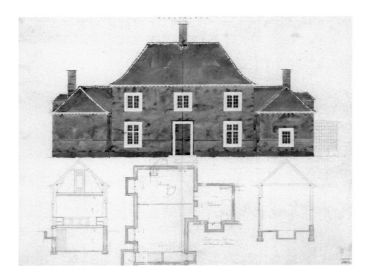

Hand drawing by Vilhelm Lauritzen. In 1922, the recently appointed medical superintendent at the Filadelfia epilepsy hospital in Dianalund asked the young Vilhelm Lauritzen to design a new residence for him. Lauritzen placed this building at the highest point of the hospital grounds and gave it a strictly symmetrical and sober expression towards the north, where visitors would see it, and a more unceremonious, welcoming look on the more private southern side. Lauritzen achieved the clear symmetry by placing the wing across from the garage in two low buildings with the main door in the middle of the axis of symmetry.

Kolonien Filadelfia, medical superintendent's residence,
1924, Dianalund

In 1926, Vilhelm Lauritzen and Frits Schlegel designed the Universal Lamp for Fritzsches Glashandel (Fritzsche's Glassware Shop). It was presented at the 1929 Barcelona International Exposition, where it won a gold medal.

The Universal Lamp, 1926, in collaboration with Frits Schlegel for Fritzsches Glashandel

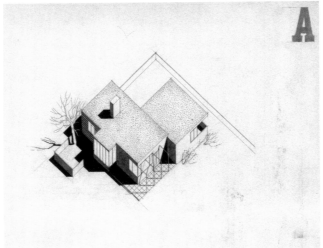

In 1933, Dansk Cement Central held a competition promoting the use of reinforced concrete in housing construction. Vilhelm Lauritzen submitted several proposals, one of which won an honourable mention.

Competition for concrete housing, 1933, Competition proposal

Nursing home for Dansk Travselskab (Danish Harness Racing Association) in Charlottenlund. A simple and well-proportioned building with a clear and distinct tactile expression.

Nursing home commissioned by Dansk Travselskab, 1934, Charlottenlund

Vilhelm Lauritzen designed a summer cottage for himself and his family in Tibirke Bakker. The house was built from timber and had a thatched roof, as prescribed in the local building regulations. At the summer cottage, Vilhelm Lauritzen pursued his hobby as a butterfly collector.

Summer cottage, 1937, Tibirke Bakker

In 1936, Vilhelm Lauritzen won the competition for a new town hall in Gladsaxe and was also in charge of the expansion in 1953. The town hall was designed to be modern and democratic. He organized the building as two reversed Ls, with the council hall placed in between the two short wings. He pulled the elegant semi-cylindrical end wall and the low wall in front all the way to the edge of the street as a way to naturally draw visitors into the square in front of the building. As in many of his projects, Lauritzen also designed the interior, favouring honest, straightforward materials such as red brick, limestone and cork, with doors and furnishings in elm.

Gladsaxe Town Hall, 1937, Søborg

In 1936, Copenhagen Airport held a competition for the first designated airport building. The winner was Vilhelm Lauritzen. In order to fully understand how groundbreaking the building is, we must see it in the context of its time. The 1930s were a time of transition for architecture, which had long focused on form and ornamentation. When Lauritzen created the terminal in 1936, his design was based purely on the building's functions, which makes it one of the earliest and most consistently modernist masterpieces in architecture history. Lauritzen, who was generally known as unassuming, humble and rational, described the vision that guided his design of the new airport terminal as 'a young and vital achievement, still to a great extent at a growing age, in which an expression of life, a wealth of as yet unrealized potentials, a certain festive optimism that is linked with things in the process of developing were the characteristics that were to make an impression on those who saw the building and moved around in it', as quoted in *Vilhelm Lauritzen: A Modern Architect* (1994). Below, a section drawing from the competition proposal. The terminal is constructed of a system of round, free-standing columns in reinforced concrete placed in a five by six-metre modular grid. This approach allowed for a large, uninterrupted and flexible arrival and departure hall.

The Vilhelm Lauritzen Terminal, 1939, Copenhagen

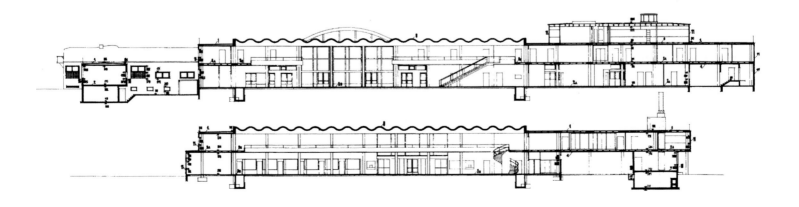

Vilhelm Lauritzen was known as a master of details. Behind the door handles, a steel plate prevents finger rings from scratching the door, and towards the airfield the radiators are concealed above the glass doors. The characteristic undulating ceiling, which appears to float above the open, pillarless space, consists of 12,500 fibreboard sheets, whose shape, materiality and perforation ensure excellent acoustic properties in the vast hall. The photo shows the railing in brass, one of the few recurring exclusive materials in an otherwise low-budget building. When the terminal was completed in 1939, commercial air travel was still a novelty, and there was no model for what an airport should look like. The functionalist Lauritzen divided the building into airside and landside sections. Entrance and traffic were handled through or along the landside section, while aeroplanes and gates belonged airside. Today, this is how most airports around the world are designed.

The middle image shows construction workers casting the undulating structure in reinforced concrete, which is only 12 centimetres thick. The airport terminal soon became a local attraction, where people came to see the 'silver birds' take off and land and to enjoy a meal in the restaurant. On the right, a hand drawing by Vilhelm Lauritzen from the 1936 competition proposal.

88

In 1943, Vilhelm Lauritzen proposed an urban development with a row of tall, south-facing housing blocks on the highest spot along the sports grounds in Gladsaxe Municipality. The development was not realized until 1968 by two former employees of the architecture firm Povl Ernst Hoff and Bennet Windinge.

Master plan for the Høje Gladsaxe housing development, 1943, Søborg

The Radio House on Rosenørns Allé in Frederiksberg from 1945 is an internationally recognized Gesamtkunstwerk. Like the airport terminal, it is a listed building. The exterior wall of the concert hall elegantly follows the interior and is a sophisticated example of construction technology. The construction is based on the shell principle with an exterior carapace that is just 12 centimetres thick, as evident in the parabolic copper roof, which is seen here with landscape architect G. N. Brandt's rooftop patio in the foreground. The different building volumes and their functions are clearly indicated in the large complex.

The Radio House, 1945, Frederiksberg

The concert hall inside the Radio House was constructed as a funnel in order to distribute the sound from the orchestra evenly to the 1,058 auditorium seats. The entire hall is lined with wood, and all the seats are upholstered with light brown oxhide. Lauritzen's grandchildren have explained that he continued to attend the weekly Thursday concerts at the Radio House throughout his life. During its development Vilhelm Lauritzen visited nine European cities in order to study the three main elements of radio broadcast buildings: concert hall, offices and sound studios. His also had a deep interest in nature and found inspiration in its clean, organic shapes, which is often evident in his works. Here, we see the small lamps inside the concert hall, which have clear references to lily of the valley.

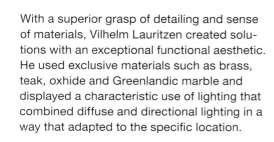

With a superior grasp of detailing and sense of materials, Vilhelm Lauritzen created solutions with an exceptional functional aesthetic. He used exclusive materials such as brass, teak, oxhide and Greenlandic marble and displayed a characteristic use of lighting that combined diffuse and directional lighting in a way that adapted to the specific location.

Lauritzen's facade proposal for
Domus Medica at Amaliegade 5 in
central Copenhagen.

Domus Medica, 1946, Copenhagen

P. M. Daell was the founder of Daell's
Department Store. He and his wife are buried
in Hørsholm Cemetery in a family burial plot
designed by Vilhelm Lauritzen.

P. M. Daell's burial place, 1948, Hørsholm

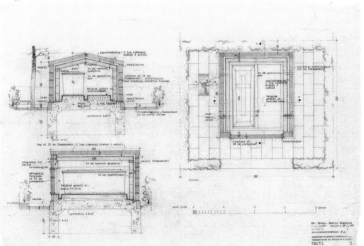

The 'new' Shell Building from 1951 is located on the corner of Kampmannsgade and Nyropsgade in Copenhagen. It was designed by Vilhelm Lauritzen as a replacement for the former building, which was bombed by the Royal Air Force in 1945 after the Gestapo had seized the building and turned it into its Danish headquarters. The recessed windows and spandrel panels in Lauritzen's office building underscore the grid structure of the facade. There is a petrol station on the ground floor. Today, the building serves as Denmark's largest shared office space. It was restored and refurbished by Vilhelm Lauritzen Architects in 2022.

The Shell Building, 1951, Copenhagen

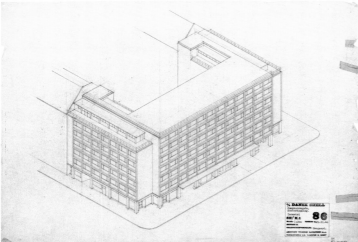

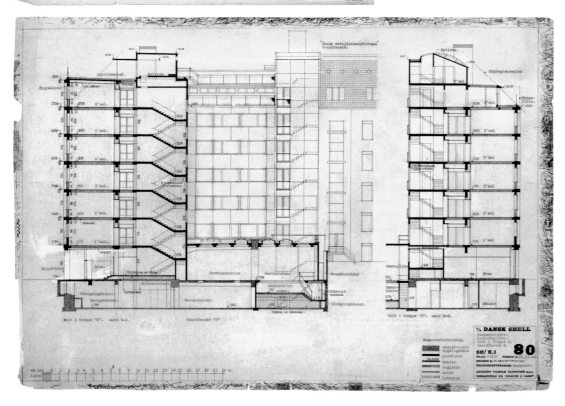

Stengård Skole in Gladsaxe
was designed during the war,
in 1942, and its architecture
reflects both the general
shortage of materials and its
adaptation to the surrounding
suburban neighbourhood. These
considerations motivated the
use of local materials such as
brick and timber and the design
of low buildings in a staggered,
intersecting arrangement with
inspiration from the Swiss
Bauhaus architect Hannes
Meyer's school in Bernau from
1927. Material shortages were
also the main reason why the
school was not finished until 1952
– 10 years after the design was
completed.

Stengård Skole, 1952, Gladsaxe

Hand-drawn elevation of the facade for
The People's House, now known as the
concert venue VEGA. The People's House
was constructed in 1953–56 for Arbejdernes
Fællesorganisation (the Federation of
Workers), which used the building for
meetings, conferences and events. The
members of the association could also rent
the place for private events.

The People's House, 1956, Copenhagen

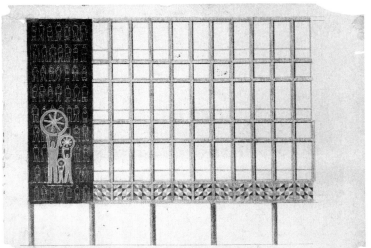

As in his design of the Radio House, Vilhelm Lauritzen used exclusive materials such as brass and teak in The People's House and also incorporated his distinctive mix of directional and diffuse lighting to strike a mood and provide functional illumination. The pattern has become a core aspect of the building's brand.

The almost labyrinthine double stairs are designed to lead large numbers of people quickly and effortlessly to and from rooms and halls on the various floors in separate flows. As he did in most of his projects, Vilhelm Lauritzen designed both the building itself and the interior, including the lamps and furniture.

On Bernstorffsvej in Hellerup, Vilhelm Lauritzen designed two houses, one for his wife, Ingeborg, and himself and one for his daughter and her family. The facade is fairly closed towards the street and more open towards the sheltered garden.

Own double house, 1956, Hellerup

After the success of the first airport terminal, Vilhelm Lauritzen was also chosen to design the new international terminal in 1955.
This time, the goal was to achieve a high degree of flexibility to enable the building to accommodate future expansions as air travel grew more popular. In 1960, the new building was completed and is still in use today, as Terminal 2.

Terminal 2, 1960, Copenhagen

'The Ministry for Foreign Affairs asked me to arrange the furnishings and that it should represent modern Danish design. I felt that it was a very demanding job, which could be better done if I asked my friend Finn Juhl – who, I think, is known also in this country [USA] as a very fine designer – to take over the most important part of the job, the furnishing of the residence. I am glad he did it, and I feel he has done a very fine job.'

– Vilhelm Lauritzen in his speech at the official opening of the Danish Embassy in Washington, DC, commenting on his collaboration with Finn Juhl, who was employed at Lauritzen's firm in 1934–45.

The Danish embassy in Washington, DC, from 1960. Again, Lauritzen demonstrates a basic functionalist approach in a design where the different functions are clearly expressed in the building's exterior walls. The chancellery is more reserved, while the ambassador's residence has a richer expression with balconies, sliding doors, shutters and free-standing columns. The exterior appears simple, light and welcoming, and both the interior and the exterior are covered with Greenlandic marble.

The Danish Embassy in Washington, DC, 1960, Washington, DC, USA, in collaboration with The Architects Collaborative (TAC) under the leadership of Walter Gropius

2860 Søborg – right until the last few years of the past millennium, this was one of the best-known postal codes in the country due to the many competitions and other programmes involving audiences participation by mail. It was part of the address for Danmarks Radio's TV-Byen with the office high-rise on Mørkhøjvej as its iconic landmark. The competition was won by Vilhelm Lauritzen Architects under the leadership of chief architect Mogens Boertmann.

TV-Byen, 1964, Søborg

The Radio Council held its meetings on the top floor of the office building in TV-Byen in Søborg. The council hall was built in 1971 after the completion of the office building.

The council hall, TV-Byen, 1971, Søborg

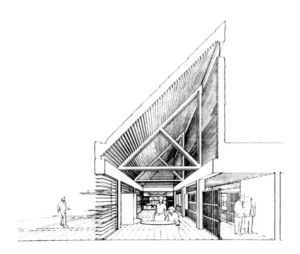

From 1978, Danmarks Radio had regional radio buildings constructed throughout Denmark. The first of these was built in Rønne, followed by Aabenraa, Vejle, Aalborg and Odense. The buildings were designed as typified building structures with a plan concept based on two parallel functional bands, one containing offices and the other containing studios and production rooms.

Regional radio buildings, 1978-, throughout Denmark

Over the years, countless passengers have
sat in the Series 38/39 Chairs in Copenhagen
Airport while waiting to board a plane.

Series 38/39, 1982

Nyhavn 4 in Copenhagen. Designed as an
infill, it is one of the narrowest buildings in
Copenhagen. It contains offices and meeting
rooms and is connected to Nyhavn 2 via door
openings in the firewall.

Nyhavn 4, 1987, Copenhagen

Louis Poulsen produced the Studio Lamp in 1988–94 as a table lamp in two sizes and as a floor lamp. The series was designed by architect and partner Jens Ammundsen.

The Studio Lamp, 1988, produced by Louis Poulsen

The former tuberculosis sanatorium on Fjordvej in Kolding was renovated and transformed into the Hotel Koldingfjord. After extensive refurbishment and the addition of an annex, the building now has 116 rooms and a conference centre with capacity for 550 participants.

Hotel Koldingfjord, 1990, Kolding

In the early 1990s, Shell held a competition for motorway facilities in the most recently constructed section of the Danish motorway system. Vilhelm Lauritzen Architects won the contract for 4 of the 14 motorway facilities, which are still in use today, on Zealand, on Funen and in Jutland. The facilities are designed with a clearly marked separation between lorries and personal vehicles and between kiosk and restaurant patrons. The different sections are tied together by 'floating' roofs that are lit from below at night.

Motorway facilities for Shell, 1991, Skærup, Karlslunde and Kildebjerg

The housing development Havrevangen in Hillerød consist of 50 non-profit dwellings constructed as some of Denmark's first low-energy housing in timber after Vilhelm Lauritzen Architects won first prize in a Nordic idea competition on low-energy construction.

Havrevangen housing development, 1994, Hillerød

In 1996, the Royal Danish Academy of Fine Arts, School of Architecture (now Royal Danish Academy – Architecture) moved to Holmen in Copenhagen in the Navy's former buildings, which are listed and now fully renovated.

Royal Danish Academy of Fine Arts – School of Architecture, 1997, Copenhagen

The CPH Airport station is an underground train station beneath the airport and one of the busiest stations in Denmark. It is a traffic hub that extends the Øresund link between Denmark and Sweden and Terminal 3, constructed with two open platforms, each servicing one track.

CPH Airport station, 1998, Copenhagen

The CPH Airport station is designed to provide a natural transition between train and aeroplane. The influx of natural daylight, the materiality and the station's calm, simple space welcomes travellers with a simple aesthetic that reflects the rest of the airport. The station cuts a long, open swathe through the square in front of the airport, opens the underground up to the sky above the tracks and provides natural ventilation for the platforms.

The platforms on the CPH Airport station form a solid base in granite, the ceiling is plastered and the walls are lined with travertine, which brings a warm glow to the space. There is no advertising on the station, which is instead decorated with photographic art hung in tombac frames on the noise-dampening platform walls.

The tip of Terminal 3 lies in extension of the station with direct access up and down via stairs, lifts and long escalators. Inside the terminal, the station's infrastructural spatial and material character continues, with an emphasis on steel, glass and granite.

Terminal 3, 1998, Copenhagen

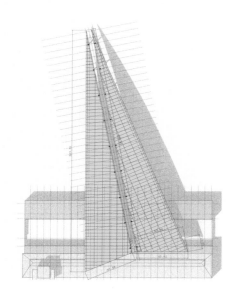

In the 1990s, it was decided to expand Copenhagen Airport to make it the traffic hub of the Øresund region. In 1998, Terminal 3 was completed, along with the CPH Airport station. The triangular plan refers to the shape of a delta wing and has given rise to the nickname 'the paper aeroplane'. The design of the terminal is classic functionalism based on an analysis of passenger types in motion: the arrivals area, which sees the largest number of people, is placed in the wide part of the terminal, the departures area is in the middle, and the station area, which has fewest travellers, is placed in the pointed end of the terminal building.

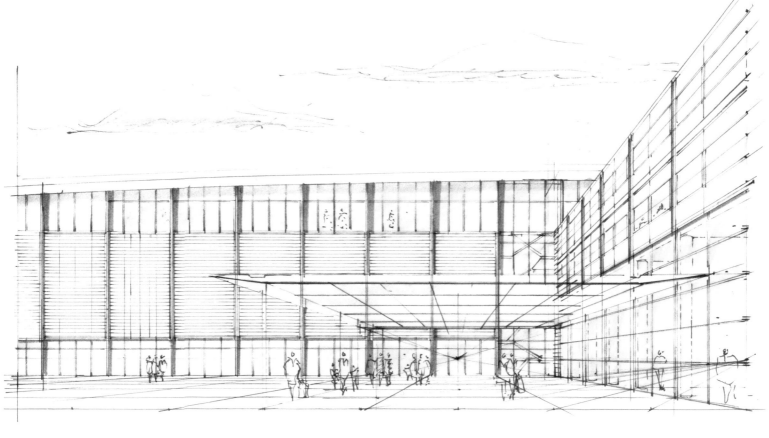

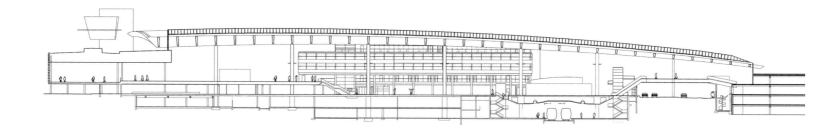

4

Functional forms

Architectural rationality and functionalism

Sprung from the modern project, modern architecture was based on a rationalist ideal from the outset. In the early 20th century, the radically modernist Austrian architect Adolf Loos launched an attack on ornament in contemporary architecture. With the modern architect's conviction that architecture plays a crucial role in people's lives and the development of society, Loos called ornament a 'crime'. In part because it was superfluous and more or less arbitrary and irrational and thus confused people's perception of the forms and properties of things; in part because it prevented architects from developing a contemporary, modern visual expression.[59]

Such a new expression was already emerging in other art forms. Above all, of course, modern, abstract visual art showed architects the way. Cubism demonstrated that the central perspective

115

which had dominated spatial perception since the Renaissance was not the only possible representation of reality, and abstract artists moved beyond nature, concentrating and focusing the expression to present reality in a version more open to human interpretation. The individual work of art also appeared more open, reflecting an autonomy which underscored that it was not primarily a depiction or a representation of nature but a work of art, an independent, human phenomenon.

Similarly, there was within architecture a growing urge to purify and focus the expression of the building's essence. In extension of the increasingly ubiquitous machine culture and new technology of industrialization, this was defined as the building's architectural *function*.

In the description of his proposal for a new zoological museum at Nørre Fælled in Copenhagen (1931), Vilhelm Lauritzen wrote: 'Display cabinets should ideally be dustproof. The more doors there are to open, and the thinner the frames around these doors are, the easier it is for dust to enter.'[60]

This common-sense attention to even the smallest speck of dust is characteristic of Lauritzen and the modern, rational approach to architecture and design in general. Indeed, this close attention to function might offer a key to functionalism in architecture. As a 'machine for living in', a building should possess the same high-precision functionality as any other machine.

In architecture, function includes first of all the building's usefulness and practical design solutions and, second, the technological development of the construction process. As for the latter, development here has followed the general trend of industrializing, technologizing and, most recently, digitizing production. Granted, the industrialization of construction is taking time and has only reached a certain level, and the reduction of craft-based practices in the construction site in favour of, for example, the use of prefab modules has not been trouble-free. However, rationalization has led to greater design freedom and, in cooperation with engineers and contractors, processes with fewer steps, well-tested solutions, a high and uniform level of quality, better abilities to 'tailor' solutions and materials, high insulation standards, lower maintenance requirements and so forth. The ideological aspects of functionalism have been toned down, while rational processes based on what works have survived the criticism, and nowadays architectural development is driven, not least, by ambitions of further digitization and expectations of more climate-friendly, sustainable solutions.

From marble and the classical orders of columns to unadorned concrete – modernism sprouts forth from its own historical foundation, here exemplified with Adolf Loos's Looshaus (1911) in Vienna. 'Like a woman with no eyebrows', some contemporary critics said of the now iconic building.

Form follows necessity

The birth of functionalism can be dated to Sunday, 8 October 1871: the night of the Great Chicago Fire. By the time the fire was put out, an unfathomable nine-square-kilometre section of the city was gone, 17,000 houses were destroyed, and 100,000 people were homeless.

Vilhelm Lauritzen's proposal for a new zoological museum in Copenhagen (1931) showcases a clarity of expression, with geometric shapes and facade features that recur in the later design of the Radio House in Frederiksberg. The proposal was never realized.

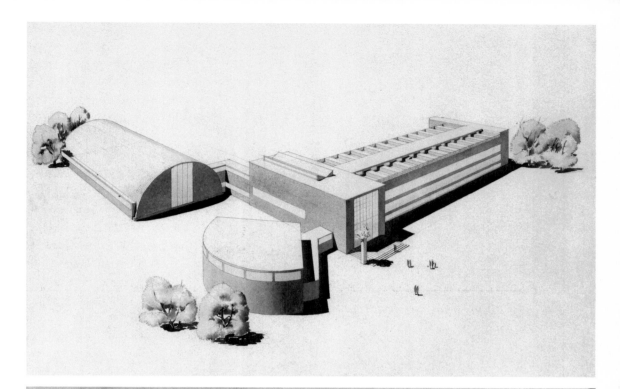

Perspective drawing of an exhibition room with dust-proof display cases and an expression of scientific rationality.

The combination of a huge need for new buildings, high land prices and the invention of the steel cage to replace load-bearing brickwork and of the lift as an alternative to stairs enabled the construction of high-rises. The steel cage provided the building's support, and the spaces in between the steel girders could be filled with brick – or with glass, which could now also be made in larger pieces.

One of the architects of the Chicago high-rises, Louis Henry Sullivan, articulated what would become the functionalist credo when he wrote these lyrical lines:

'Whether it be the sweeping eagle in his flight, or the open apple-blossom, the toiling work-horse, the blithe swan, the branching oak, the winding stream at its base, the drifting clouds, over all the coursing sun, *form ever follows function*, and this is the law.'[61]

Sullivan spent a year studying at the École des Beaux-Arts (School of Fine Arts) in Paris, where he undoubtedly encountered the work of the French architect Eugène-Emmanuel Viollet-le-Duc, whose *Entretiens sur l'architecture* was published in English in the United States in 1875. In his search for clues for a modern architecture, Viollet-le-Duc did not follow the academic tradition of turning to antiquity but instead turned to the overlooked and underestimated period in between antiquity and its Renaissance: medieval Gothic. Here he found not a style but construction principles that could be applied to modern materials, and what he wrote was as much a textbook for future architects as it was a theory of architecture.

For example, he challenges the 'vulgar error that reason stifles the imagination'. On the contrary, he says, the architect must use his judgement to arrange and order all available experience with the same care as he analyses the building programme. While artists thus previously had a style imposed on them, they must now *seek* a style. In the Greek temple, it is not style but construction that is of relevance, according to Viollet-le-Duc. In admiring a sailing ship, he says, its beauty lies in the fact that its forms seem so perfectly adapted to its function. Our epoch, says Viollet-le-Duc, by which he means the modern era, is subject to a similar 'necessity'. If an architect accepts this necessity, the architecture will have style, because it results from the application of the principle of said necessity.

Modern beauty stems from the necessity of objects or works of architecture, and although Viollet-le-Duc does not use the word 'function', the principle he repeatedly emphasizes is clearly the necessity of function. By accepting that beauty springs from necessity, we also achieve the honesty of expression that is another core concept of modern architecture:

'A thing has style when it has the expression appropriate to its uses. A sailing-vessel has style, but a steamer, which should conceal its motive-power to assume the appearance of a sailing-vessel, has no style; a rifle has style, but a rifle made to resemble a cross-bow does not.'

When the architect returns to Paris from his excursion to Greece or Rome and wishes to reproduce the ruins that seduced him, necessity would compel him to build in local stone rather than marble. Should he then build a structure that would be a 'lie in stone?' asks Viollet-le-Duc rhetorically.[62]

Around this time, the British Arts and Crafts movement was on a similar mission to preserve functional honesty by strengthening the crafts culture that was the traditional guarantor of quality but which was now facing the risk of extinction, supplanted by industrial culture and its standardized, simplified and – in the eyes of many – ugly products. Spearheaded by art historian John Ruskin, the move-

Wainwright Building (1891) in St. Louis, Missouri, USA, by architects Dankmar Adler and Louis Henry Sullivan. The building is considered one of the prototypes of the modern high-rise, but while the construction is modern, the composition, the pilasters and the frieze at the top, with its flower garland ornament, make it more a personal interpretation of classicism.

ment claimed that the alienating effect on the industrial worker of the division of labour was reflected in the impoverishment of industrial products. This was inevitable, as the worker had not actually shaped the objects and could never attain the qualified relationship with the production process that he was supposed to transfer to the product.

Finally, the standardization of industrial production also exposed the status of the worker as a standard component, replaceable and, in time, probably utterly superfluous. According to the movement, industry was robbing both worker and product of their dignity, and it was this dignity that the German architect and industrial designer Peter Behrens and the German Werkbund (Association of Craftsmen) sought to preserve in design by *designing* rather than inventing, engineering and developing industrial products.

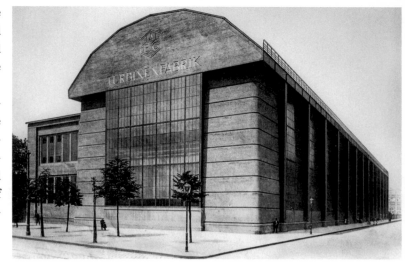

The AEG turbine factory (1909) in Berlin by Peter Behrens. The early modern architects took an interest in different types of projects than the ones that had hitherto characterized the academic tradition, and focused instead on housing for ordinary people, factories, hospitals and other everyday functions.

Meanwhile, in Copenhagen

A similar mindset was taking root at the Royal Danish Academy of Fine Arts, School of Architecture in Copenhagen around the First World War, the time when Vilhelm Lauritzen attended the Academy. Studies of style had been abandoned, and the students organized excursions into the real world to take measurements of local Danish architecture. They analysed what functions could be deduced from the buildings and generalized concrete examples into structures and approaches that could be used in the various tasks they would encounter.

The young architects were looking for the origins behind the historical styles, and they discovered that their profession required intimate knowledge of both classical and vernacular architecture. The formal and functional structures were no less present in the shape of a stone axe or a timber-frame farmhouse than in buildings or architectural principles based on academic styles. As one student, Povl Stegmann, noted in connection with a study assignment:

'It is not enough for me to know that a column has an entasis; I must have a thorough knowledge of the conditions that determine the line that seems most harmonious as an entasis. I must know these things, which are basic for all linear harmony – like prosody in poetry or time and intervals in music. I want to know what happens when one slackens a line or tightens it, know why the master of the Parthenon did not put the cornice in a completely straight line, but instead let it curve insignificantly towards the middle. It is these things that mean something for the aesthetic evaluation of art.'[63]

Around this time, a Nordic form of classicism emerged in extension of the highly evolved tradition and frank, artless national Romantic architecture. Within this neoclassicist style, as it was called, architects such as the Swede Gunnar Asplund and Danes Carl Petersen, Kay Fisker and Aage Rafn created works of classical harmony with original contributions to the interpretation and refinement of traditional architecture. Canonized examples include Asplund's Skogskapellet (Woodland Chapel), Petersen's Fåborg Mu-

The medical superintendent's residence at the Filadelfia hospital (1924). Watercolour by Vilhelm Lauritzen.

The young architects were looking for the origins behind the historical styles, and they discovered that their profession required intimate knowledge of both classical and vernacular architecture.

seum and Fisker and Rafn's Gudhjem Station. To this we might add Vilhelm Lauritzen's design of the residence for the chief physician at the epilepsy hospital Kolonien Filadelfia in Dianalund on Zealand (1924), a classicist manor house in a clear and symmetrical composition with personality and Danish national roots.

The combination of functional analysis and an open mind towards historical architecture, whether from antiquity or the vernacular tradition, made neoclassicism a perfect stepping stone to an actual modern, functionalist architecture of Nordic variety. Another important factor in the establishment of Nordic modernism was probably the fact that industrialization began relatively late in the Nordic countries. This meant that the craft culture survived for longer and led to a softer transition to industrialized construction, which only really began to gain momentum until after the Second World War.

As the modern architecture movement spread from Central Europe to the rest of the world during the interwar years, in the Nordic region it thus encountered a firmly regionally anchored classicism. The utopian movement reached the Nordic region in the late spring of 1930 with the Stockholm Exhibition's seductive, bright and airy vision of a sunlit and well-built welfare society for all. Thus, solidly founded Nordic architectural traditions and elegant neoclassicism merged with modern, functionalist rationalism. The result: Nordic functionalism, dubbed *funkis*, which must have looked rather promising under the gently billowing canopies in the summer breeze.

From the beginning, Nordic modern architecture developed in a less fundamentalist and more honestly functionalist direction, aimed not at the fashionable International Style but at a more site-specific, refined but also pragmatic common-sense architecture. As a result, 'Functionalism prevailed in the Nordic countries in a way that was not seen anywhere else', as Nils-Ole Lund concludes.[64]

Skogskapellet (1928) by Gunnar Asplund in Enskede near Stockholm, one of the most famous works of Nordic neoclassicism.

Gudhjem Station (1916) by Kay Fisker and Aage Rafn. Less well-known but just as clever in its marriage of classic proportions and the best aspects of the architectural tradition of southern Scandinavia.

Faaborg Museum (1915) by Carl Petersen. Neoclassicism as a congenial infill.

Vilhelm Lauritzen's Nordic functionalism

Vilhelm Lauritzen's first two projects, submitted for a competition on summer cottages held by *Politiken* in 1917 while Lauritzen was still an architecture student, demonstrate purposeful design in interaction with nature and site, resulting in a rationally simplified, harmonious interpretation of tried-and-tested construction in a traditional expression. 'The plans were simple, to suit life in the country for city folk. The bedrooms and the kitchen were at the ends, with a large family room in between them. Both cabins have straw hipped roofs. The walls were half-timbered, with cladding outside, plastered inside.'[65] One of the projects earned Lauritzen a second prize.

The approach, as Lisbeth Balslev Jørgensen points out, was the same as in architect Ejnar Dyggve's development plan from 1916 for Tibirke Bakker, with a strict emphasis on preserving the natural

Modern setting for contemporary art. The proposal for 'an exhibition building at Charlottenborg' in Copenhagen was awarded a gold medal (1926), in part for its functional analysis of natural daylight, which is represented with great accuracy in Vilhelm Lauritzen's watercolour.

The full-scale exhibition Weißenhofsiedlung (Weißenhof Estate) in Stuttgart. On a journey through Central Europe in 1927, Vilhelm Lauritzen saw how 17 of his best-known colleagues, including Le Corbusier, Ludwig Mies van der Rohe, Walter Gropius, Hans Scharoun, Bruno Taut and J. J. P. Oud, reinterpreted the typological category of residential architecture in a modern, contemporary and aesthetic-functional light.

feel without fencing or overhead power lines. Many Danish progressives, including architect Ivar Bentsen, writer Johannes V. Jensen, philosopher Jørgen Jørgensen and other cultural figures, built summer cottages in Tibirke Bakker. Here they formed a little colony, elite-in-nature, as captured in prickly caricature by Hans Scherfig in his novel *The Missing Bureaucrat*, which he wrote during a stay in Tibirke Bakker in 1937 (English edition 1988), the same year that Lauritzen built a summer cottage for himself in the area. The architecture nestles into the setting, displaying its kinship with the local farmhouses but condensed to achieve what would now be called minimalist simplicity: over time, the silvery weatherboarding and thatched roofs blended into the surrounding hills. The flooring was unfinished planks, with yellow tiles in front of the fireplace; the walls were lined with birch plywood boards installed with brass screws.[66] Today's best summer cottage architecture and the increasingly common natural shelters are strongly inspired by the summer homes by Lauritzen and his contemporaries.

The winning proposal that Lauritzen and his colleague and former Academy classmate Frits Schlegel designed for the refurbishment of Daell's Department Store on Nørregade and Krystalgade in Copenhagen reflects a similarly moderate rationalization of an existing structure. The proposal leaves the roof and window apertures intact but redesigns the facade to tie the buildings into a coherent structure. The renovation was so limited that the architects were not entirely happy with the result, but over time Lauritzen carried out several subsequent changes to the department store, which now appears as an excellent example of classic Nordic modernism with elegant, horizontal window bands, discreet variation in the form of staggered lines and windows that wrap around corners as bays, traditionally maritime features, such as a turret resembling a luxury liner smokestack, a flagpole and a bridge, and a light, gracious expression throughout that is, mildly put, in short supply in the genre of department stores and shopping centres.

While the first Daell's Department Store project was classicism decorated with 'architectonic lace', as arch-functionalist Edvard Heiberg observed in his review in the journal *Kritisk Revy*,[67] Lauritzen's project for an exhibition building at Charlottenborg was bold modernist monumentality with large, striking iron-frame windows set in niches of natural stone that softened the light. The building was designed and sited based on a thorough analysis of how to minimize reflections on the exhibits on display: a 'pioneering approach to the issue of daylight'.[68] The project earned him the Academy's Small Gold Medal in 1926. His proposal for a crematorium in Frederiksberg is also modern, 'matter-of-fact cubistic'[69] in a muted expression in accordance with its function without being strict or formalistic.

On a journey through Central Europe in 1927, Lauritzen visited the Deutsche Werkbund's housing exhibition with its display of full-scale houses without ornamentation, constructed with flat roofs without cornices and with large windows. Another important stop was the Bauhaus[70] in Dessau. Once Lauritzen was back in Denmark, his projects became even more distinctly modern.

His terrace house design Celotex maintains a low pitched roof, but in a clearly modernist touch, the windows are moving towards the edges of the exterior walls. His Universal Lamp (1926) with an opal glass shade and dome, which received a gold medal at the Barcelona International Exposition and represented a rational and simple lighting solution with sufficient illumination and without glare, is

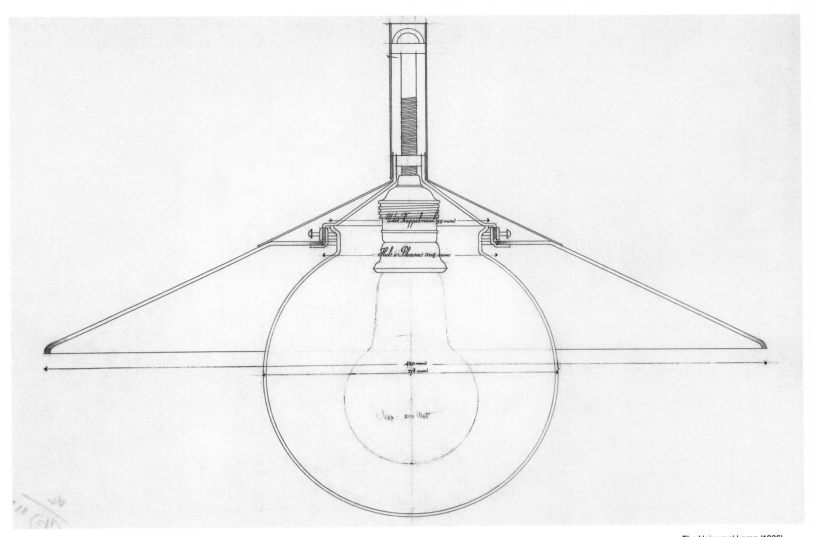

The Universal Lamp (1926). Vilhelm Lauritzen's modern functionalist lighting design, a joint project with Frits Schlegel, is a two-shade lamp constructed of a closed hemisphere of opalized glass topped by an open cone-shaped 'hat' in matt glass.

The architecture nestles into the setting, displaying its kinship with the local farm-houses but condensed to achieve what would now be called minimalist simplicity ...

Vilhelm Lauritzen's watercolour of the realized proposal for the refurbishment of Daell's Department Store (1930) on Nørregade in Copenhagen. The watercolour shows the simple functionalist facade with long, white window ribbons that appear to be continuous. Daell's closed in 1999, and the building has now been converted into a hotel, but the facade is preserved and remains in its original design.

Tuborgvej 76 (1929). The modern facade as an abstract composition based on underlying functional spatial solutions.

På Højden 15 (1933). The light character of the pavilion serves as the basis for a functional dwelling.

in close dialogue with both the Danish designer Poul Henningsen's lamps and the Bauhaus lamps.

In 1923, Lauritzen was in charge of the reconstruction of the playhouse Nørrebros Teater in Copenhagen, which had been destroyed by fire the previous year. In this project he once again demonstrated his exceptional grasp of spatial qualities as well as his technical skill and creativity. Everywhere, the new medium of film now called for existing theatres to be able to function as cinemas or 'movie theatres'. Building on the existing, narrow plot, Lauritzen increased the height of the building, added a horseshoe-shaped balcony to the auditorium and placed the lobby and vestibule under the new, more steeply sloping floor. As an added benefit, this also brought the entrance to the theatre up to the street level. The design met the client's brief of expanding the number of seats by more than 800, to 1150, with every seat facing the stage. Again, his approach was functionalism applied with scientific precision:

'The sloping walls on the sides of and above the proscenium and the angle of the underside of the balcony are designed to optimize the acoustic properties. The calculated reverberation times are as follows: empty hall: 1.7 secs.; 1/3 full: 1.4 secs.; full occupancy: 1.1 sec.'[71] In a review in *Architekten* [*sic*], his former teacher Edward Thomsen described the design of the theatre as a 'technical miracle'.[72]

The house Lauritzen designed for his brother, Otto, on Tuborgvej 76 (1929) in Copenhagen demonstrated what Fisker, C. F. Møller and Stegmann famously had done in their recent design of Aarhus University: create modern architecture in yellow brickwork. Lauritzen's design was an asymmetrical composition with steel-framed windows and clear-cut, geometric semicircles for the staircase and canopy designs. His proposal for a new zoological museum in Nørre Fælled in Copenhagen (1931) was geometrically well ordered and functionally motivated with a varied use of rectangles, fan shapes and a hangar form. The project was never realized, perhaps because of its uncompromising approach. His design for a detached house at På Højden 15 in Gentofte (1933) was almost as flat as an abstract painting by Mondrian. The house uses right angles throughout, 'even for the gutters', as Lisbet Balslev Jørgensen notes.[73] His contribution to Dansk Cement Central's competition for the use of reinforced concrete in housing construction, which was not yet allowed according to the Danish building regulations, shows rational and relevant functionalist considerations that go far beyond the specific project: spatial functions, flexibility and economic calculations are all carefully weighed and considered.

Wireless and weightless

The construction of two of the newest and most groundbreaking phenomena of the modern era became Vilhelm Lauritzen's principal achievements: the first terminal for Copenhagen Airport (1939) in Kastrup on Amager and the Radio House (1941/45) in Rosenørns Allé, Frederiksberg. The buildings were to replace existing structures: an outdated airport building known as the Wooden Palace, which looked like something that belonged in a holiday camp,[74] and the broadcasting corporation's building at the Danish Royal Theatre, known as the 'nest box', with impossible acoustics. The two projects epitomized the modern, international world that rational, functionalist architecture was associated with. The functionalist approach was the obvious choice here, as the development of modern technology meant that 'functional requirements were the same everywhere', as architecture historian Jørgen Sestoft notes. The projects were intended to set the bar in their respective areas:

'In around 1930, neither functional, technical nor aesthetic schools had yet been created with a joint conception of what broadcasting buildings or airport terminals should look like. The rapid development of these media prevented the creation of types. Each time a new building was ready, progress had been made and the experiences that had been gained were often negative. [...] [It] was Lauritzen's lot to be the one in Denmark who concretized how these commissions were to be designed, commissions for which there were no traditions, ones that were specifically modern and highly extrovert. There were many modern schools, residential buildings, and office buildings, but "Radio Building" and "Airport" are referred to in the nominative singular.'[75]

Today, as instant, electronic communication and global aviation seem commonplace, it might be difficult to imagine the wireless and airborne revolution that ushered in the modern age around 1900. At the time, the prospects must have seemed literally dizzying. Wirelessness continues to revolutionize our lives to this day, and weightlessness has an air of eternity about it – freedom from gravity bears more than a little resemblance to the Messianic utopia of freedom from death, eternal life.[76]

Watercolour by Vilhelm Lauritzen for the competition for the first airport terminal at Copenhagen Airport (1939).

Radio and aviation

On 12 December 1901, the Italian physicist Guglielmo Marconi received the world's first transatlantic wireless radio signal. Originating in Poldhu, Cornwall, the signal was received in St. Johns, Newfoundland, where Marconi had travelled in order to experience the result of his invention first-hand. This first radio broadcast was fairly modest in content: it consisted of the Morse code sequence for the letter 's'. Of course, that small 's' was a signal with far-reaching consequences. Two years later, on 17 December 1903, on a plain outside the small town of Kitty Hawk in North Carolina, USA, the American brothers Wilbur and Orville Wright kept an aeroplane in the air for 59 seconds, thus making the first sustained flight.

Initially, the main role of radio technology was as a means of communication for ships – and aeroplanes – but from the early 1920s, broadcasting services provided radio broadcasts for everyone with a

The first airport terminal building (1939) was constructed on a fairly limited budget with little room for the use of exclusive materials. Among the most expensive materials was the Greenlandic marble used for cladding the arrivals area and the teak used to frame the glass doors. The project had a budget of 700,000 kroner but ultimately came to 1,000,000 kroner, as minor expansions proved necessary. Here, the terminal space is seen towards the arrivals hall with the iconic undulating ceiling made of perforated fibreboard.

The distinction between local and global began to change radically when the telegraph and the radio began to deliver news of events on the other side of the planet virtually the moment they occurred.

wireless receiver. Thus, the BBC also has its centenary in 2022, and Den Danske Statsradiofoni (Danish State Broadcasting Service), later Danmarks Radio and now DR, was founded in 1925.

Until after the First World War, aviation had been the reserve of daredevils and air force pilots. In fact, the basis for civilian air travel was the large number of aeroplanes that had survived the war and lacked a purpose when the war ended in 1918. In Denmark, Det Danske Luftfartsselskab (the Danish Aviation Company) was promptly formed, and two years later the company opened the route Malmö-Copenhagen-Warnemünde. Still, air travel remained an exclusive mode of travel: the route was serviced by an open seaplane with room for two passengers.[77]

Radio broadcasting and aviation undoubtedly had a greater impact on our sense of time and space than Einstein's theory of relativity. Until the modern era, the instant simultaneousness that we now take for granted was limited to local and tangible phenomena. Both distant news and people travelled slowly, as they always had. Until the late 19th century, most of the people in the world thus travelled at the pace of a pedestrian or a horse-drawn carriage. The distinction between local and global began to change radically when the telegraph and the radio began to deliver news of events on the other side of the planet virtually the moment they occurred. In an aeroplane, it was even possible to reach the site of the event quickly.

The airport

The same year as the Danish broadcasting service began its transmissions, Copenhagen Airport moved from its previous location in Kløvermarken to its current one in Kastrup. Shortly after the move, *Politiken* wrote:

'Everyday life in Kastrup Airport is becoming increasingly European. Within about half an hour every morning, Air Expresses depart for Berlin, Amsterdam, Hamburg and Paris – and every hour throughout the day, aeroplanes land carrying passengers from every corner of Europe. [...] Copenhagen celebrities took their seats in the cabin of the Paris Express. And six hours after Jabiru rounded the City Hall tower, its propellers spun near the beautiful steel column of the Eiffel Tower. Breakfast in Copenhagen, lunch in Amsterdam, afternoon tea in Paris, plenty of time for a stroll in the boulevard before dinner and a visit to the opera – what an adventure! Even Hans Christian Andersen's imagination fell short when he wrote about air travel half a century ago.'[78]

In 1936, the Danish Ministry for Public Works announced an architecture competition for a new terminal building for the airport, which Vilhelm Lauritzen won. His airport terminal from 1939 is now tucked away out of sight, and for some time it remained a forgotten gem in Danish architecture. Low, white, light, transparent, almost fluid, it appears as a pavilion in the spirit of the Stockholm Exhibition or as one of the luxury liners that were so admired by modern architects, complete with railing and striped 'smokestack'.

The thin floors of the two-storey building are supported by free-standing round, slender white columns. The central departure hall has a double ceiling height and is covered by an undulating roof in reinforced concrete, cast in situ and lined with tiles. The ceiling has the same function of bracing the construction as a traditional use of girders would have had but appears as a lightweight, free-floating element. Indeed, it is only 12 centimetres thick despite its span of 12 by 45 metres. The main facade has long, low horizontal window bands, interrupted at the entrance by a canopy extending 6 metres out and seemingly floating above arriving travellers, almost as if it were made of canvas. The impression is white and airy, like laundry swaying in a summer breeze.

At the time, both the undulating roof and the canopy were praised for their bold use of the relatively new material of reinforced concrete, but in fact the canopy is a hollow case constructed around load-bearing iron girders and lined with Eternit on the underside.

In the terminal's restaurant section the curvy facade, with lightly framed glass from floor to ceiling, provides a liberating break from the stricter geometry of the main facade and offers a panoramic view of the runway. The constructive virtuosity of the building is due, not least, to Lauritzen's collaboration with the project engineer, Christian Nøkkentved.

The terminal was clearly carefully planned and designed in every detail. The layout of the central hall, with its asymmetrical counter, is an exemplary demonstration of how to achieve good traffic flow in an airport, including guiding passengers in the right direction, even if they are not familiar with the terminal.[79]

The design variation in materials, composition and rectilinearity alternating with free forms, which makes the space an echo of movement, like frozen music or ballet, is characteristic of the ease with which the functional and constructive aspects are executed in the best examples of early modern architecture. This artistically inspired but user-friendly execution, which rarely resorts to formalism or mannerism, is so characteristic of the Nordic version of the architectural modernism that Vilhelm Lauritzen was such an early exponent of that it is not too much to join Jørgen Sestoft in calling his assessment that the airport terminal 'presages a special, modern form of expression: a Nordic one. Both Asplund and Aalto delivered similarly 'undogmatic interpretations of Modernism' but not until later.[80]

The Radio House

While Lauritzen's airport terminal is virtually secret, the Radio House is, by contrast, indisputably his best-known work of architecture. Hundreds of radio employees have had it as their daily workplace, and thousands of people have visited, not least for perfor-

Following spreads:

The entrance to the concert hall foyer is highlighted with a canopy covered with timber battens and fitted with custom-designed lamps designed by Vilhelm Lauritzen. The facade is clad in light sandstone.

The concert hall inside the Radio House, with an audience capacity of 1,058. The funnel shape ensures high acoustic quality everywhere in the room. Panels and battens are lined with the lighter maple, while the rest of the hall is built in darker Oregon pine. The seats are aged, light brown oxhide.

The Radio House (1945) in Frederiksberg. Watercolour by Lauritzen.

133

The lamps, wall treatments, furniture and all other details, down to the bridgeboards, banisters and door handles, make a coherent whole, as if they had grown out of it in a single organic design process.

mances in the popular concert hall during the many years when it was the main building of Danmarks Radio (from 1964 along with the headquarters TV-Byen (TV City) in Gladsaxe, designed by Vilhelm Lauritzen's employee Mogens Boertmann) until 2007, when both radio and TV production moved to Ørestad in buildings designed by Vilhelm Lauritzen Architects, among others. The address of the Radio House, Rosenørns Allé, was familiar to generations of radio listeners and closely associated with the broadcasting service. Today, Lauritzen's building houses the Royal Danish Academy of Music.

In November 1935, after a lengthy preliminary process – impacted also by the failure of Stærekassen (1931), which from the outset proved both too small and acoustically impossible – involving both intense public debate and internal disagreement in the Radio Council, the Council decided on a proposal from a small selected project team with Lauritzen as architect and Nøkkentved as engineer. The proposal was approved by the Danish Parliament in spring 1936. Apart from a few reductions, including the elimination of a 125-metre-tall TV tower, it was built almost exactly in accordance with the original design: an administration wing in staggered volumes and two heights towards the street linked with a lower studio block in the courtyard and a fan-shaped concert hall. One of the office blocks is pulled back from the street, making room for an entrance area with a canopy. The concert hall, with its distinctive trapezoid, curved roof, has a separate entrance in the side street it faces. It too is pulled back from the street to form a small urban space with plane trees. The composition is clearly related to some of the finest, groundbreaking modernist projects of the time, including Le Corbusier's project for the building for the League of Nations in Geneva from 1927.

Inside, all the furnishings were designed by the architect himself in collaboration with the Danish furniture designer Finn Juhl, who was an employee of Lauritzen's at the time. The lamps, wall treatments, furniture and all other details, down to the bridgeboards, banisters and door handles, make a coherent whole, as if they had grown out of it in a single organic design process. Not least the lamps, including the Radio House Pendant, are rightly recognized as design classics today.

Because of the war and the German occupation of Denmark, the Radio House was not inaugurated until September 1945. An official opening event during the latter part of the occupation, when all public life in the country was under German control, would invariably have been turned into a Nazi propaganda show, which the Danes were keen to avoid. In the late summer after liberation, there was no trace of former reservations in the reception of the building in the Danish press: 'A dream in light colours and bold lines', 'overwhelmingly beautiful yet homely, luxurious and intimate at once', 'a brilliant fairy tale of art and skill'.[81]

The foyer of the Radio House in 1945. The ceiling is covered with rectangular fields of oxhide – apart from one piece which has been left in its full animal shape. To tease him, Poul Henningsen called it 'a waste of sole leather'. Vilhelm Lauritzen replied that 'gilding fades, but sole leather remains', adding, 'It creates a surface in a sound-absorbing covering of frames and mineral wool. I could have used cheesecloth, oilskin, or several other things, but believed that leather would improve with the influence of light and air and take on a beautiful color and fabric-like character with time'. The quotations are taken from duelling opinion pieces in LP Nyt from 1941, pp. 54 and 69 and quoted from *Vilhelm Lauritzen: A Modern Architect* (1994). Note also the curved schedule, which lets the guests read the bottom lines without needing to bend their backs or knees. Lauritzen's design of furnishings for the Radio House also included bespoke furniture for the foyer.

A terminal for the International Style of the 1960s

After the war, it was clear that Lauritzen's beautiful airport terminal was undersized for the rapidly growing number of travellers, which had tripled from 45,000 a year. Lauritzen prepared several proposals for new terminals, an expansion project began in 1955, and the new Terminal 2 was ready in 1960. In a new organization of the traffic flow, travellers and baggage were now sent to separate levels. Baggage was briskly and efficiently handled at ground level, while after check-in, travellers took the escalator to the first floor and went to the gates in the so-called fingers. The same principle is still in use today, with certain modifications, in Copenhagen Airport and, indeed,

Not long after the official opening of the first airport terminal in 1939, the number of travellers passing through Copenhagen Airport began to grow in reflection of the spread of the jet engine. In 1960, the new, flexible and future-proof international terminal opened, which is still in use today, as Terminal 2.

After dropping off their luggage, travellers continue up to the first floor and the gates. Vilhelm Lauritzen marked this functional shift by switching from sandstone floors to plank floors and by going from double to single ceiling height. The intention was to convey a sense of homeliness and of being a passenger – an approach that has since been copied in many other airports.of the jet engine. In 1960, the new, flexible and future-proof international terminal opened, which is still in use today, as Terminal 2.

most airports the world over; it seems fair to say this quintessentially functionalist solution has proven quite successful.

However, the architecture critic for *Politiken* Svend Erik Møller was so vexed by the journey inside the airport that he wrote about a 'disharmonious symphony on the theme of climbing and descending stairs'. He also felt that there was 'almost a more welcoming feel in the waiting room at the Main Train Station'[82] than in Lauritzen's building, which is a rational boxy design, related to Arne Jacobsen's contemporary SAS Royal Hotel in Copenhagen, Skidmore, Owings & Merrill's Lever House in New York and many other high-rises in the International Style, which came to dominate the second phase of modernism that unfolded after the Second World War. Seen from outside, it could have been almost any office building from the period, with its smooth curtain-wall facade, window bands and coloured patches in a neutral blueish grey, perhaps with inspiration from the play of light in a water surface or a sky with drifting clouds, everything strictly rectangular. However, inside the departure hall, which is one big room with escalators, a mezzanine with backstage access to the shopping centre and the fingers with gates and boarding, one experiences the powerful impression of the free space in its span between columns and facades, a modern cathedral feeling, the ceiling three storeys overhead with the round 'full moon' skylights that the firm has made a theme in subsequent expansions of the airport.

Møller's grumpy review did not remain uncontested. In an editorial in *Architekten*, Poul Erik Skriver retorted that Møller's scathing assessment of 'a work of architecture that any architecture connoisseur will rate highly' only demonstrated the critic's unsophisticated view of modern architecture and revealed 'an aversion to familiarizing himself with this area of the arts. He has failed to develop a proper understanding of the modern expression'.[83]

This little dispute reflects what we might call modern architecture's image problem. It has far-reaching consequences if a fairly public art form, such as architecture, can only be discussed internally among confirmed 'architecture connoisseurs' and requires 'familiarity with the expression' to be appreciated. If the aesthetic of modern architecture is so alien to common mortals, the very concept of the modern project has failed. Indeed, in the most pessimistic assessment of modern architecture, that has been the conclusion: cold, lacking in popular appeal and functional in name only. The flat roofs could never be made leakproof and they let in the rain.

A connoisseur such as Vilhelm Lauritzen's colleague and former employee Hans Erling Langkilde had a very different assessment of Lauritzen's approach in general and the specific result of the analysis of the particular task:

'Lauritzen accepts that architecture must be created on contemporary terms and also openly acknowledges that it must thus be an expression of its time. It would be not just dubious but downright dishonest if it were to ignore the factors specific to its time. He was the first to articulate the point of view, which has since been widely quoted, that functionalism introduced a new moral more than it introduced a new style or aesthetic. It is honest and courageous, particularly of an aesthete, to so clearly assign priority to the ethical requirement: unconditional respect for the task and its conditions. [...] The new airport building meets the demands of the task and its time. The hall demonstrates a new leap in spatial perception: the space is defined less by its exterior delimitation and more by the internal organization of the functions; an "open form", flexible, diverse.'[84]

Hand-drawn perspective of Terminal 2 from 1955. Vilhelm Lauritzen designed the building as a steel construction, without a centre, with circular skylights that throw rhythmic patches of daylight onto the light-coloured sandstone floor – an interpretation of the paving outside and a hardwearing surface capable of standing up to trolley cases and shoes.

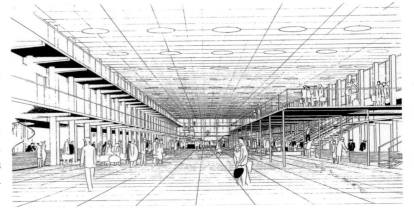

A third terminal for a pragmatic time

Vilhelm Lauritzen Architects also won the competition for the next expansion, Terminal 3, which was completed in 1998, when air travel had become a widespread mode of transportation. That year, 16.8 million travellers passed through Copenhagen Airport, an average of 45,000 a day. By 2018, the annual number had reached 30 million. The modern dream of weightlessness had become reality. Air travel had become commonplace.

Perhaps that marked the end of dreaming. Certainly, towards the end of the 20th century, the modern project was declared dead, and modernism was considered obsolete or undesirable, or both, within all art forms, not least architecture. In the meantime, criticism of modern architecture, even from the 'connoisseurs', with significant contributions from, especially, the United States during the 1960s and 1970s, was gaining momentum as part of a general revolt against the modern project as a whole, which from the late 1970s was relabelled 'postmodernism'. The main thrust of the criticism was a call for acknowledging that a 'postmodern condition' had replaced modernity, and that the modern project and its utopia was therefore out of step with the actual conditions of life and thinking, not least as they appeared in the light of globalization and the drastic expansion in electronic information and communication, which in the meantime has only accelerated further.

However, the postmodern diagnosis of society met with widespread scepticism, and postmodernism as a classification of architectural style never really caught on. It seemed there was a deeper reason why modernism had abandoned historical eclecticism with its liberal mix-and-match of all stylistic features, which the postmodernists were now trying to reinstate.

Perhaps the reason was that modernity *is* a project, which people have learnt to live with in all its frustrating incompleteness. No longer as an enthusiastic, revolutionary departure from all aspects of historical legacy and unquestioning excitement about machines, mobility and mass production but rather as a pragmatic acceptance of a development that, with consistent fine-tuning of the control mechanisms of social engineering, will, nevertheless, always be on the way towards something better. A process that is still managing to revolutionize itself, as proven by unbelievably transformative information technology.

The modern project had in fact changed, and pragmatism appeared to be a key concept. In the clash between modernists and postmodernists in the 1980s and 1990s, both sides had a point. Modernity could no longer survive as a utopia; on the other hand, for better or worse, it had now become reality. For all its shortcomings, the modern world was actually working. This was the new reality to be acknowledged, for society at large as well as for architecture, which as an applied social art form usually finds itself in the middle of the current.

Terminal 3, Copenhagen Airport (1998). A delta wing connects metro station, departures hall and arrivals hall.

Modernity could no longer survive as a utopia; on the other hand, for better or worse, it had now become reality.

Terminal 3 from the 'kiss and fly' side.

The airport looks like an aeroplane

Terminal 3 is shaped like a fighter plane or like a child's folded paper plane. The shape thus refers directly back to the ideas that define the origins of modern architecture, according to architecture historian Emil Kaufmann: the work of the French architects of the Enlightenment Ledoux, Boullée and Jean-Jacques Lequeu and the notion of *architecture parlante*, 'speaking' architecture, based on the notion that a building can convey an idea, for example by resembling what it is 'about'. The concept was not formulated until a hundred years later, in the mid 19th century, as a satire on the zany ideas of 'revolutionary architects'.[85] However, their radical departure from the large imposing designs of the baroque and their Counter-Reformation urge for ornamentation, sensuous qualities and illusionist effects could arguably be seen as an attempt to arrive at the forms themselves in their inherent, geometric nature.

'Autonomous' is how Kaufmann described the principle of the new architecture, with its pavilion structures, clearly separate and identifiable buildings and building components in clear-cut forms, as easily decoded as road signs. He even saw Ledoux's architectural method as a reflection of the spirit of the Enlightenment: 'At the same time as the rights of the individual were enshrined by the Declaration of Human Rights, at the same time as the German philosopher Immanuel Kant founded autonomous ethic to replace the old, heteronomous moral, Ledoux laid the foundation of autonomous architecture.'[86]

The wing shape of Terminal 3 suggests free, autonomous play with forms, although, naturally, it is not entirely free. The architects explain that the triangle shape is functionally motivated and point to the specific feature of airport architecture as something that is experienced from several different vantage points. In addition to our standard vantage point, a little over one and a half metres above the ground, it is also perceived from the airline traveller's bird's-eye perspective.

Apart from that, an airport terminal is mainly experienced from inside. This experience can be slightly claustrophobic, precisely because air travel became such an overwhelming success. For many years, for example, the terminals in the airports Heathrow in London, Charles de Gaulle in Paris, Arlanda outside Stockholm and Kastrup in Copenhagen were reduced to shopping centres with acute constipation. This was in stark contrast to the new-built exceptions to the rule, including the airport in Barcelona, with its soaring ceiling height, and the one in Zurich, with its soothingly discreet acoustics, engineered with Swiss perfection.[87]

Thus, the functional rationale for the terminal design is perfectly justified. Like motorways and railway stations, airports are, above all, spaces we move through, in large numbers, and the ability of the structure to facilitate good flow is crucial. Møller's dissatisfaction with the stairs and escalators in the new Terminal 2 revealed that he had no understanding of flow, since, in fact, he disliked both airports and air travel. As he wrote, 'There is probably no mode of transportation that is more cumbersome or more uncomfortable'.

Simple logic and
care for functionality

The triangular shape of Terminal 3 addresses the difference in the number of people who pass through or briefly spend time in the different sections of the building. The wide end of the triangle has to accommodate all travellers. The departure area is placed in the middle section, which about 40 per cent of the departing passengers pass through. Finally, the station area, designed for the approximately 15 per cent of the passengers who were expected to take the train, is placed in the pointed end of the triangle.

According to the architects, they sought to continue 'the simple logic' from the first airport terminal, the material selection from Terminal 2 and the light and the spacious hall from the old railway stations. Thus, there is a nod to the facade of Terminal 2 in the internal facade of the inserted mezzanine on the east side of the building. Also, the large glass lobby at the widest part of the triangle evokes the station atmosphere of the railway era but without the icy draughts, smelly fumes and unforgiving acoustics. On the contrary, the space has a surprisingly relaxed and informal – some might say typically Danish – atmosphere, which helps take the edge off the stress of travelling and the somewhat contrived air of anodyne international cosmopolitanism that many airports have. It works, thanks to the architects' care for functionality.

It is a pleasant space to be in. In fact, it might almost be nicer if it was even bigger and if it was not, like all public spaces, overgrown with vending machines and signs and waste bins and other clutter. It is a space for people in a hurry, and it can clearly handle the rush, even if the journey still, as described in Svend Erik Møller's rant about Terminal 2, takes travellers up and down a few stairs or escalators. The hall is at ground level, and security and transit hall are one level up, as is the metro station, since this section of the metro line is elevated above the motorway and the access road to the airport; travellers meanwhile have to go one level down to get to the train station for the line up the coast or over to Malmö. The station, too, was designed by Vilhelm Lauritzen Architects.

Just like the old railway halls, Terminal 3 is a building that is almost only experienced from inside. However, travellers who arrive by taxi or bus or are dropped off by a car – and who are not in too much of a hurry – may notice how the up to 20-metre-tall glass sides of the 'jet plane' that culminate in an independent architectural point are shored up against the wind with buttresses placed in a rhythm matching the distribution of the columns supporting the roof. The sense of classic harmony, embedded and freely interpreted in a modern idiom, is quite in the Vilhelm Lauritzen's spirit.

Architect and Vilhelm Lauritzen expert Morten Lund aptly characterized this spirit in a defence for the huge task of moving the old and not very well-preserved airport terminal to a new, safe home several kilometres away:

'The architects of the '30s described themselves as functionalists and awarded themselves the role of social constructors of a society in the making. Although many of them were self-assured gentlemen, the idea of striving for immortality by erecting monuments in glass and concrete struck them as absurd. They spoke with great precision about their works and about the latest new developments in

Terminal 3 seen from the first floor just above the arrivals area. The skylights in the terminal provide daylight and facilitate wayfinding to the metro station and access to the platforms.

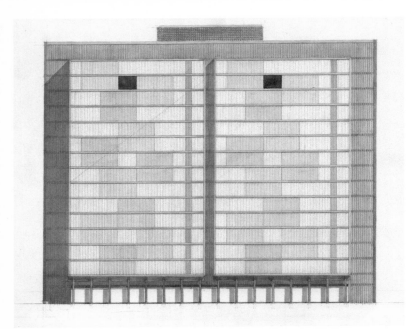

TV-Byen (1964) in Gladsaxe. Coloured facade drawing showing its abstract composition.

fire safety, district heating, rubbish chutes and ventilation systems. However, they used words such as architecture and art gingerly.'

The wider historical context that the airport terminal is a part of renders it indisputably worthy of preservation – as a work of architecture and as a work of art: 'The enthusiasm for the new technology, the liberation of humanity and the global community has survived as a palpable power in the old modern spaces. Here, the beginning of our own time lies preserved.'[88]

TV City and DR City

When television came to Denmark in the early 1950s, the Radio House had to be expanded, but it quickly became clear that the new cuckoo would soon outgrow the building at Rosenørns Allé. Thus, in 1964 it got a nest of its own in the former wetlands of Gyngemosen in Mørkhøj, Gladsaxe Municipality, just outside Copenhagen. Both Vilhelm Lauritzen and his closest employee, Mogens Boertmann, took part in the architecture competition, and the choice fell on Boertmann's project.

The new complex was named TV-Byen, an apt name for the sprawling facility, which consisted of a collection of low, connected, staggered buildings with courtyards containing everything needed for TV production – studios, workshops, room for broadcast vans, costume department and so forth as well as an 18-storey office tower. Later, a news building was added to accommodate the evening TV news and other shows, which were not moved to Gyngemosen until 1983.

The architectural expression of TV-Byen is dominated by the office tower, which was also designed by Vilhelm Lauritzen and which was originally visible from afar, from its position in the sparsely built-up area high up in the open landscape near the Hillerød motorway. Since then, the area has become completely built-up. Probably in an effort to lighten the facade, it was divided in two. The horizontal window bands, which fill out the space between the floors, have a fairly dense pattern of vertical light grey sunshades, occasionally interspersed with bands or patches of other colours in a discreet, abstract composition.

In the early 1990s, the Danish Parliament decided to try to breathe life into the country's languishing capital, which was burdened by debt and unemployment, by launching three giant projects: a combined bridge and tunnel link across Øresund to Sweden, a new district called Ørestad on Amager and a metro to improve Copenhagen's tired public transport network. The funding followed the British New Town principle, meaning that the metro would be funded by revenue from the increased value of the land that the metro would produce in Ørestad. In order to kick-start the sale of land and give the new district a strong core of public institutions, it was soon decided to build new facilities for DR in Ørestad. This would also put an end to the increasingly impractical physical separation of radio and TV production and the growing online media in a new media house.

146

The sunshades in TV-Byen form
the facade's varying abstract
colour pattern – an active
facade long before this concept
became trendy.

Vilhelm Lauritzen's design of the Radio House in Frederiksberg during the 1930s led to a long-standing historical collaboration between Danmarks Radio (now DR) and Vilhelm Lauritzen Architects. At the turn of the millennium, DR wanted to bring all the corporation's TV, radio and concert facilities together under one roof and launched a major international architecture competition. Each participant submitted an anonymous proposal for a master plan for a 125,000-square-metre multimedia building. Vilhelm Lauritzen Architects won the competition with a project aiming to create a city in the city – a kasbah consisting of four buildings, each with its own identity.

'It looks almost exactly like
our competition project, so
we really can't complain.'

The project came to be seen as one of the major scandals in Danish public construction due to massive budget overruns in connection with the construction of the concert hall and the resultant sacking of DR's managing director followed by significant cutbacks in staff to make ends meet. Numerous inquiries were carried out to identify where the blame lay, but one thing was clear: it was not the fault of the architects.

The result of the architecture competitions required four architecture firms to work together: the French architect Jean Nouvel won the contract for the concert hall; the Danish firm Gottlieb Paludan Architects would build the section for administration, internal service and canteen; another Danish company, Dissing+Weitling architecture, won the commission for the news building; and Vilhelm Lauritzen Architects would design the TV production building and the master plan for the whole complex. The key feature of the master plan is the unifying 'interior street', designed to tie together the four different architectural expressions in both function and form.

For practical reasons, the TV production building is necessarily a fairly closed structure but with a tall ceiling and similarly tall light apertures, which makes for a very dramatic influx of daylight, matching the drama of the productions. A similar sense of drama is found in the shiny black tile cladding on the studio blocks and the deep red colour of the studio towers, echoing DR's logo. With walls in raw polished concrete, the materials, colours, combinations and contrasts continue modern architecture's spiritual affinity with the colours and dramatic statements of expressionist art but in a contemporary interpretation matching contemporary smooth, shiny and often black electronic media devices – modern media technology, congenially combined with the necessary architectural, rational functionalism in a highly complex workplace, where technical and human processes constantly need to come together with split-second precision and focus.

The functionalist profile of DR Byen was also updated to include the sustainability dimension, an inescapable concern in contemporary construction, and meet current environmental standards. Climate and energy optimization was considered for all materials and solutions. The studio blocks are carefully positioned to shield direct sunlight in order to prevent overheating of the offices. The double exterior walls allow fresh air to circulate naturally thanks to the 'chimney effect', rainwater is used to flush the toilets, and the building harnesses the natural cooling effect of groundwater.

In light of the scandal, it may be worth pointing out another aspect of some significance: often, an architectural design undergoes considerable modifications from competition project to finished building. But not in this case; on the contrary. In terms of both design and budget, the project hit the target precisely. 'It looks almost exactly like our competition project, so we really can't complain', said a visibly pleased Thomas Scheel in a TV interview.[89]

DR Byen's 'interior street'. Light and shadow effects varying between giving the impression of a pergola and a city street. The red studio towers of DR Byen are part of the classic media tricolour of black, white and red and also signal 'Recording!'.

The future of technological functionalism

With three or four generations of Copenhagen Airport terminals and three generations of radio and TV buildings, Vilhelm Lauritzen Architects had almost become 'house architects' in the two key modern institutions of aviation and electronic media in Denmark. Many commissions were won in competition with other firms, but over the years the firm has clearly developed a sense of familiarity with large public projects and the implied need for architectural solutions that balance rationality and humanism. However, projects that are subject to both intensive use and broad public scrutiny continue to call for contemporary interpretations of functionalism.

A balanced approach based on the integrity that comes with experience thus shapes most of the projects designed by Vilhelm Lauritzen Architects. In response to the criticism of functionalism and modern architecture, rather than turning to catchy slogans or a quest to create the next 'iconic' work of architecture, the firm prefers to point to a concrete practice based on an undogmatic, contextually sensitive wholeness of form and function. Forms that function.

In addition, the firm cultivates critical self-reflection and concern for what sort of development of civilization they are deeply and concretely involved in designing, in both form and function – a constant and healthily cautious engagement with rationality and its strongest weapon, technology. Is functional technology going to help us progress into the future, or will we be drowning in the consequences of climate change long before we can get there?

Vilhelm Lauritzen Architects strives to maintain the balance between necessary modern technology optimism and, behind it, contact with what is essential. As partner and CEO Gyrithe Saltorp puts it: 'Digitization should free up energy so we can focus on designing even better architecture projects.'

For example, the firm works with so-called parametric design and artificial intelligence, using simulation to optimize the sustainability of the projects. It is obvious that artificial intelligence is a technology that can lead straight to the alienating independence of machines: a new fate. However, architects also need to be able to navigate in the general current of market economics and societal development that all modern construction is subject to: 'Our digitization level is fairly high, but construction is developing at a rapid pace. That's why we want to be good playmates for the most visionary actors in this field. [...] I am a huge fan of those of our employees who work with digitization. I love their ideas, even if I honestly don't always get them', says Gyrithe Saltorp.[90]

The ceiling of Terminal 2, Copenhagen Airport (1960). Rhythmically spaced skylights bring daylight into the deep, oblong building.

2000–

2000	Copenhagen Business School
2005	Trekroner Skole
2009	DR Byen
2016	Krøyers Plads
2021	LIFE Campus
2025	New North Zealand Hospital

Copenhagen Business School on Solbjerg Plads forms an active urban space in an interplay with Frederiksberg Library and Frederiksberg Gymnasium (Frederiksberg Upper Secondary School). The narrow buildings towards the south and the skylight bring daylight into the building, suspending the boundary between indoors and out. The school features quality materials that can stand up to extensive daily wear and tear.

Copenhagen Business School, 2000, Frederiksberg

The Nordic Embassy was built after the civil war in 1992 with the aim of contributing to the restoration of the country and the development of its fledgling democracy. The building design was inspired by the experimental period of modern architecture in Mozambique during the 1950s and 1960s and by the work of the Portuguese architect Álvaro Siza (b. 1933). The construction draws on technical solutions developed by the American architect Louis Kahn (1901–1974).

Nordic Embassy in Mozambique, 2000, Maputo, Mozambique

Tuborg South is the maritime district in Hellerup between Strandvejen, Tuborg Boulevard and Dessaus Boulevard, developed in collaboration with Carlsberg after the relocation of the Tuborg brewery.

Tuborg South, 2001, Copenhagen

The Nyx Lamp, which was launched in 2004 in collaboration with Focus Lighting, is one of Denmark's most popular contemporary streetlight designs. The lamp is cast in aluminium and characterized by producing a high, efficient and glare-free diffusion of light.

The Nyx Lamp, 2004, in collaboration with Focus Lighting

Trekroner Skole is a reinterpretation of a traditional Danish school. There are no corridors, and all the classrooms are large and well-lit. All the classrooms have direct access to the centrally placed 'garden of knowledge', which serves as a shared learning environment. Each classroom further opens onto a local square with seating plinths.

Trekroner Skole, 2005, Roskilde

With a height of 72 metres, the control tower is a landmark in the flat landscape on Amager. It consists of a flat base building, a 21-storey stem and, on top, the cab, where the air-traffic control operations are carried out. The tall stem is made of slip-form cast concrete, while the cab is made of steel and faceted glass panes with its broader side facing the runways. Inside, the floors are made from hardwood timber.

Control Tower, 2005, Copenhagen

The 34 terraced houses were inspired by the architecture of a traditional English village. To ensure variation, the houses are staggered in relation to the street and have varying spatial qualities. A peek down the narrow access street that branches out into paths shows varied facade compositions with sheltered courtyard gardens.

The houses on the former barracks site in the town of Farum form a dense structure, which appears as a homogenous whole, even though it consists of individual dwellings. The simple whitewashed exterior walls with hardwood cladding show a Nordic modernist streetscape with references to the layout of a traditional English village.

The Regiment Park, 2006, Farum

The characteristic roof of the clubhouse wraps around the building with a white steel frame that is intended as a reference to the ships in the harbour. The large window sections provide a view of the harbour environment and Øresund.

Clubhouse for Royal Danish Yacht Club, 2007, Hellerup

The Copenhagen Airport metro station is a traffic hub that provides easy access to airport hotels, parking and other facilities. The metro station extends the longitudinal axis of the airport terminal with skylights. In order to avoid columns, which would obstruct the passenger flow, the load-bearing constructions are placed in the outer construction that support the tracks.

Copenhagen Airport metro station, 2007, Copenhagen

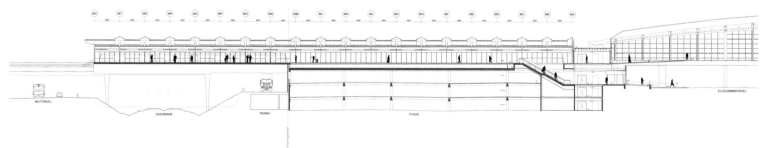

Waterfront Shopping, Hellerup's largest shopping centre, is located in the Tuborg Harbour area and offers a mix of shopping options and business facilities. It is designed to open towards the harbour and has references to a box being opened.

Waterfront Shopping, 2007, Hellerup, Carlsberg Properties A/S in collaboration with Braaten+Pedersen ApS

When Danmarks Radio moved to DR Byen, the beautiful media building on Rosenørns Allé was available for new activities, and in 2008 the Royal Danish Academy of Music moved in.

Royal Danish Academy of Music, 2008, Frederiksberg

In order to enable Philip de Lange's listed building from 1750 on Gammel Strand to accommodate both current and future requirements, Vilhelm Lauritzen Architects added new exhibition facilities, improved access conditions and made room for new functions, such as a book café and a multipurpose hall.

Contemporary art and design centre Gl. Strand, 2008, Copenhagen

The folded construction forms a protective screen around the building. In the gap between the screen and the building itself, small patios and covered outdoor spaces emerge that offer an excellent sheltered nook, not least for persons with mobility impairments, as there is no change in level in the transition between indoors and out.

Symfonien nursing home, 2008, Næstved

The acclaimed Danish architect Henri Glæsel designed Tuborg Bryghus (Tuborg Brewhouse) in the Tuborg Harbour neighbourhood in 1903. The last beer was brewed in the old copper kettles in 1996, and in 2005 Carlsberg Properties sold the building, which was subsequently restored and converted into offices.

Tuborg Bryghus, 2008, Hellerup

DR Byen is based on the notion of creating a city in the city, featuring four buildings inspired by a North African kasbah, each building maintaining its own distinct expression but joining with the others to form a unified complex. The intentions of Vilhelm Lauritzen Architects' master plan were realized by the three Danish architecture firms Vilhelm Lauritzen Architects, Dissing+Weitling architecture and Gottlieb Paludan Architects together with NOBEL arkitekter and the French architect Jean Nouvel.

DR Byen, 2009, Copenhagen

163

Punkthusene is a cluster of three characteristic seven-storey office buildings in the Tuborg Harbour neighbourhood in Hellerup. Their organic shapes and shades of white and blue were inspired by Øresund. The facades have no vertical elements.

Punkthusene, 2009, Hellerup

Stævnen is the last housing block in Ørestad South, overlooking Amager Fælled and Køge Bugt. Towards the south, the building grows to 11 storeys, hence the name Stævnen (the Bow), as on a ship. Staggered open and closed balconies and variations in building height create dynamic facades and allows for rooftop patios and dedicated views of nature.

Stævnen, 2009, Copenhagen

The clubhouse in Fælledparken is a reinterpretation of the older, white painted pavilions located around the park in Copenhagen's Østerbro district. From its weighty underground base, the house twists its way through the grass of the park. The mound that the clubhouse rests on was modelled out of surplus soil from the construction. This avoided the economically and environmentally costly process of removing the soil and instead utilized the waste to create nice low hills for soaking up the sun.

Clubhouse in Fælledparken, 2011, Copenhagen

Skovhuset (Forest House), Centervænget 43–45, consists of 104 assisted-living dwellings and a centre comprising two to four storeys placed towards the wood and the central woodland lake.

Skovhuset, 2013, Hillerød

Vilhelm Lauritzen Architects resides in a former warehouse that the firm refurbished. The building's raw interior qualities have been preserved as a nod to its industrial past. The legacy from Vilhelm Lauritzen remains subtly present in the open and welcoming rooms as well as in the small details.

Pakhus 48, 2014, Copenhagen

Frikvarteret in Copenhagen's Nordhavn
district was converted from a smithy
servicing the area's maritime industry to
a development of small terraced houses.

Frikvarteret Housing, 2015, Copenhagen

On Fælledvej 6 in Slagelse lies the psychiatric
hospital, a modern treatment facility with
194 individual patient rooms, a psychiatric
emergency room and a knowledge centre.
Here, light, art and architecture are important
aspects of the treatment.

The psychiatric hospital in Slagelse, 2015, Slagelse, in
collaboration with Karlsson Architects

167

Krøyers Plads is the central part of the Copenhagen harbour front. The square has three long individual buildings ranging from four to six storeys in height, interwoven with the historical warehouse environments. The geometry and materials clearly refer to the setting, but the buildings' contemporary expression makes them landmarks in central Copenhagen. Vilhelm Lauritzen Architects and GHB Landscape Architects (now LYTT Architecture) developed the preliminary project, which was incorporated into the detail plan. The subsequent design of the square and the buildings was carried out in collaboration with Cobe.

Krøyers Plads, 2016, Copenhagen, in collaboration with Cobe and LYTT Architecture

168

Illum is one of Denmark's oldest and best-known department stores. Since 1899, Illum has had a prominent position on a corner of Amagertorv, and in 2016 its facade was redesigned to refer to the historical setting – like a townhouse that clearly shows its structural composition: base, mid-section and roof.

Illum Department Store, 2016, Copenhagen

Marmorbyen (Marble City) in Copenhagen's Nordhavn district is a housing development in a green setting in the middle of the harbour. The two islands with their 259 dwellings draw inspiration from the coastal nature on Zealand with small dunes and hardy plant species. The design creates urban spaces between the buildings that encourage active use.

Marmorbyen, 2016, Copenhagen

Housing development in Skousbo near Viby Sjælland with 110 non-profit dwellings in a construction system with load-bearing elements of solid timber and facade cladding in slate and wood.

Skousbo 1 + 2, 2017, Viby Sjælland

The European School Copenhagen on Ny Carlsberg Vej in the heart of Carlsberg Byen, surrounded by heritage buildings listed as worthy of preservation, is a modern school that acknowledges its historical environment. The familiar gold discs from the old storage cellar built in 1969 and designed by architect Svenn Eske Kristensen inspired the golden facade elements, and the characteristic protruding bricks on the facade are a reflection of the ornamentation on the historical buildings.

The European School Copenhagen, 2018, Copenhagen, in collaboration with NORD Architects

Danish modernism in New Delhi. The embassy balances an open and welcoming appearance with a discreet, nearly invisible layer of strategically positioned security. It acts both as a hub for culture and Danish entrepreneurialism and as a residence for some of the Danish diplomats.

The Danish and Icelandic Embassy in India, 2019, New Delhi, India

The non-profit housing estate Skademosen near Roskilde consists of two horseshoe-shaped buildings. The human scale, the sensuous surface of the wood and the slightly staggered building elements give rise to intimate courtyards that invite the emergence of a social community.

Skademosen Trekroner, 2019, Roskilde

Copenhagen Airport consists of three terminals with a number of 'fingers' (piers) conveying travellers to and from the gates. Pier E is the largest expansion of Copenhagen Airport in 25 years. It is designed as a series of interconnected spatial flows bathed in natural light. With floating footbridges lined with ash and supplemented with concrete cast in situ, integrated works of art and marble terrazzo floors, it comfortably guides travellers through the large complex.

Pier E, 2019, Copenhagen, in collaboration with ZESO Architects

Surrounded by former warehouses, the new housing on Pier 2150 is situated directly on the waterfront in Copenhagen's Nordhavn district. The 68 owner-occupied flats are designed to balance the interplay between the former industrial and warehouse area, the residents' need for privacy and the public's access to the harbour.

Pier 2150, 2020, Copenhagen

Snedkerhuset (Carpenter House) is a student residence. Its interior and exterior industrial character refers to Valby Maskinfabrik (Valby Machine Works), which was located in the area. The detail image shows the building's organic facades clad with red brick veneer.

Snedkerhuset, 2021, Valby

The design of the day-care facility Bøgelunden combines the latest educational knowledge with employees' requests and professional input. It has a capacity of 150 infants and preschool children distributed in four large 'home groups' with a large, integrated outdoor space with access to the first floor via a play ramp.

Bøgelunden, day-care centre, 2021, Blovstrød

Fortkaj in Copenhagen's Nordhavn district is a modern interpretation of the classic perimeter block that is so common in central Copenhagen. The housing complex consists of four angled buildings with alternating smooth or relief brick exteriors and distinctive white window niches and red window frames.

Fortkaj, 2021, Copenhagen, in collaboration with Cobe

Famous and infamous, the Danish national rail company DSB's former freight-railway building from the 1960s occupied Kalvebod Brygge 32 and was an unusually pure manifestation of the Brutalist style that most people either loved or hated. Now, the 180-metre-long building, nicknamed KB32, has been transformed into a six-storey open office space. From the outset, the vision was to reuse the dilapidated building, which has been carefully wrapped in delicate matt aluminium elements – a much more climate-friendly solution than demolition.

KB32, 2021, Copenhagen
Bottom: The facade as it looked in 1967, 2018 and 2021

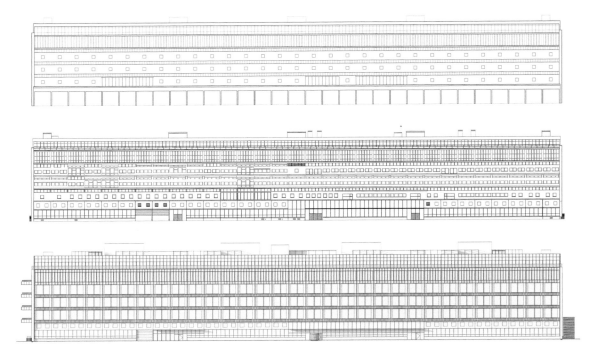

Steno Diabetes Center Copenhagen is Northern Europe's largest hospital for the prevention and treatment of diabetes. With input from the world of science, the building redefines the typological category of 'hospital'. The building's core is a garden on two levels with small niches and varied plantings. Inside, all the communal and waiting areas have been rethought to create a hospital that promotes healthy living and converts waiting time into active time with a focus on diet, exercise and learning. Wood is used as the primary interior material, including on the warm wooden floors and ceilings, because studies have shown that the presence of wood helps reduce stress.

Steno Diabetes Center Copenhagen, 2021, Herlev, in collaboration with Mikkelsen Arkitekter and STED

Ninety-six columns in raw oak welcome visitors to the LIFE Campus, a visionary national learning centre for children and youth aiming to inspire interest in the natural sciences. In the middle of the former hunting grounds near Lyngby, the building manifests the interplay of nature and science combined with a digital learning environment that includes high-tech laboratories, a 360-degree projection auditorium and modern workstations.

LIFE Campus, 2021, Lyngby, in collaboration with LYTT Architecture

On a hill outside Roskilde lies a non-profit housing development with 67 dwellings in timber buildings. The buildings were designed for Boligselskabet Sjælland (Sjælland Housing Association) in a system based on cross-laminated timber – CLT Flex – where all the building models were designed as 3D models, which were then produced as elements in solid cross-laminated timber ready to be assembled on site. The system was developed by Vilhelm Lauritzen Architects in a partnership with other companies with the purpose of creating good, functional, flexible and affordable homes.

Toppen, 2021, Roskilde

The Niels Bohr Building is one of Denmark's biggest construction projects ever. The design is based on a vision of bringing different disciplinary environments together in borderless communities and to create a building that promotes the emergence of knowledge across organizational boundaries. The building has 130 laboratories and accommodates seven thousand students and more than a thousand researchers.

The Niels Bohr Building, 2022, Copenhagen, in collaboration with Christensen & Co Architects

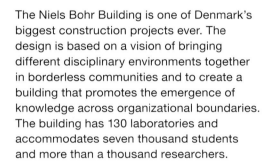

As in many of his projects, Vilhelm Lauritzen designed everything for The People's House (1956), from chairs, tables, wooden panels, friezes and chandeliers to fittings, door handles and power outlets. As he saw it, it was the details that really made the big difference and shaped the larger whole. To mark Vilhelm Lauritzen Architects' centenary, some of his furniture designs have now been put into production for the first time in collaboration with Carl Hansen & Søn, which produces the furniture by hand on Funen. Shown here is the VEGA Chair, a functionalist design based on the dimensions of the human body. The chair has Vilhelm Lauritzen's characteristic organic expression and one of his typically uncompromising details: small oak feet.

The VEGA series, 2022, in collaboration with Carl Hansen & Søn

178

Vilhelm Lauritzen also designed the interior for the Radio House (1945). His best-known design is the Radio House Pendant, which was found in many homes throughout the second half of the 20th century. The pendant was relaunched by Louis Poulsen in 2016. As with the VEGA Chair, Vilhelm Lauritzen Architects has pulled out the old sketches, drawings and prototypes and has put his Foyer series from the Radio House into production for the first time in collaboration with Carl Hansen & Søn to mark the firm's centenary. Both the easy chair and the sofa are held together by two brass screws, one on each side.

Foyer series, 2022, in collaboration with Carl Hansen & Søn

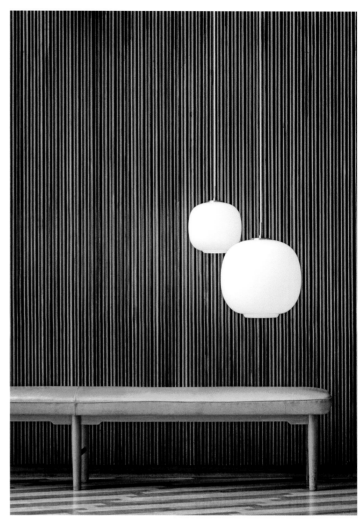

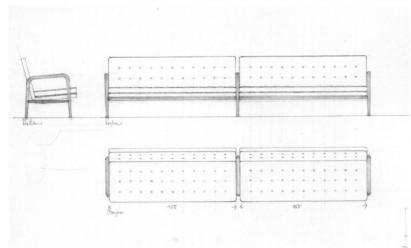

Kronløb Island in Copenhagen's Nordhavn district (2023) will be Denmark's 432nd island. Its design draws on inspiration from the calcareous deposits by Stevns Klint (Stevns Cliff). The island appears as a monolith rising out of the water. It contains both private homes and a public urban space.

Kronløb Island, 2023, Copenhagen, in collaboration with Cobe

At a height of 60 metres, the Tip of Nordø (North Island) is Copenhagen's new landmark, a contemporary lighthouse on a striking scale at the entry to Copenhagen Harbour. The functional design is based on an hour-by-hour simulation of the weather over the course of a year, which made it possible to design and place the geometrically faceted window elements strategically so they reduce the direct influx of sunlight based on their orientation.

Tip of Nordø, 2023, Copenhagen, in collaboration with Cobe

Trælasthuset is a new parking structure in Copenhagen's Nordhavn district with an exterior of cork and recycled aluminium. The proposal, which also included a facade cladding consisting of a pixelated relief, won an open project competition held by CPH City and Port Development in autumn 2019.

Trælasthuset, 2023, Copenhagen

'Vitality' was the guiding vision behind New North Zealand Hospital, designed by the Swiss architecture firm Herzog & de Meuron and Vilhelm Lauritzen Architects – a vision which insists that there is more to life than just being alive. Like the Steno Diabetes Center Copenhagen in Herlev and the psychiatric hospital in Slagelse, this project too aims to challenge the traditional role of hospitals in society and shift the emphasis from a narrow focus on treating disease to a broader goal of promoting good health. The hospital building is mostly low, largely restricted to just two storeys, with private wards throughout. There is a good influx of natural light, wood is used as the main material and there are views of either the central garden or the surrounding landscape. Wood is a recurring element in both the interior and the exterior. Soft shapes, daylight and the view of the open landscape create a homely atmosphere where nature is always present.

New North Zealand Hospital, 2025, Hillerød, in collaboration with Herzog & de Meuron

Nordic nature becomes a recreational element in the new expansion of Terminal 3 in Copenhagen Airport, where travellers after the tax-free zone are met by a lush, open garden and a central square that offers a good overview and great views of the runways. With inspiration from the Vilhelm Lauritzen Terminal building from 1939, the ceiling is undulating and perforated, letting natural light into the building.

Terminal 3, expansion, 2028, Copenhagen, in collaboration with ZESO Architects

5

Enlightened communal space

Enlightenment for freedom

The freedom that the modern project promises can only be partially achieved through the construction of the welfare state and functional settings. A tenet of modernity which has gradually come to appear as a given is that freedom is something we need to invent for ourselves – in a sense, every moment of our lives, as long as we continue to learn and experience. The success of the modern project relies to a high degree on the development of social-mindedness in a democratic, enlightened context. We are continually nurturing this social-mindedness in each other and, not least, in our children. It is a reassuring aspect of modern rationality that new little humans increasingly, and in growing parts of the world, can expect to grow up in a fairly enlightened communal space.

The modern project takes its concept of freedom from the Enlightenment, conceived and written with a capital E in the mid 18th century by free-thinking intellectuals with a degree of curiosity that could almost be characterized as modern. A typical product of their curiosity was the *Encyclopédie ou dictionaire raissoné des sciences, des arts et des métiers*,[91] a comprehensive catalogue of the facts and skills that might educate someone who had broken free from religious dogma, superstition and myths. It was a book intended for the *citizen* in a new, growing social class of independently working and thinking individuals who insisted on having rights, not just as citizens and members of a social rank but simply as human beings.

These were the people Kant had in mind when he defined enlightenment as 'the human being's emergence from his self-incurred minority'; 'self-incurred' in the sense that one does not dare to trust one's own reason and instead relies on what others say, whether they represent religion, authorities or the state or simply claim to know best in order to fan their ego or because they are selling something. '*Sapere aude!* Have courage to make use of your *own* understanding! is thus the motto of enlightenment', Kant wrote.[92]

The modern notion that enlightenment produces not only more knowledgeable and cultivated people but also *better* people, who by virtue of their knowledge and cultivation will do the right thing, is closely related to its foundation in a society of socially minded citizens.

This means that civilization, the continuous edification of the citizens and continuous rational, functionalist, scientific, technological, social and welfare progress are the conditions of the modern project's success. Progress is not brought about by technology, machines, robots and clever solutions alone but is a result of the cooperation of enlightened community members. The free exchange of opinions and ideas in society and in communities helps to fine-tune both the enlightened individuals and the machinery of society as a whole and its political, ethical and aesthetic gears.

The Danish communal space

It is hardly a coincidence that the finely woven democracy and small, homogenous society of Denmark is characterized by widespread popular engagement in organizations. Individualization, the growth of globalized subcultures and social media may threaten this volunteer engagement in associations. However, even if communities take different forms, not least shaped by a growing role of social media interactions, our society still appears to have a strong need for the formation of a communal identity or 'schooling', in a broad sense, that characterizes the project of enlightenment.

This also implies a constant need for physical settings for schooling and education. Naturally, this core area of modern architecture is also represented in the practice of Vilhelm Lauritzen Architects. Schools and, in particular, buildings for science education and research are thus a significant part of Vilhelm Lauritzen

Trekroner Skole (2005) near Roskilde. No long corridors, no overpowering scale. Instead, direct access from the classroom to the play area in the playground.

The modern notion that enlightenment produces not only more knowledgeable and cultivated people but also better people ...

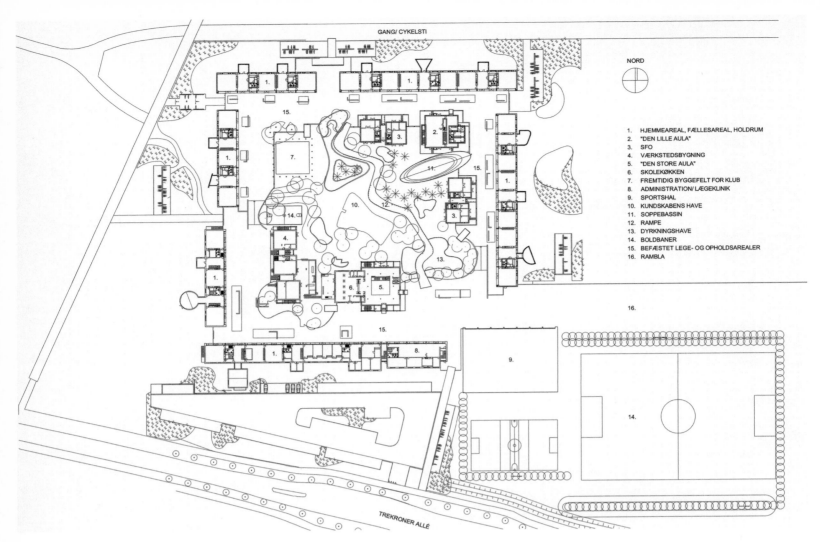

Site plan for Trekroner Skole.
Notice the atrium structure,
the extent of the garden within
the overall complex, the small
school's separate lobby and
the 'garden of knowledge' in
the centre.

NORD

1. HJEMMEAREAL, FÆLLESAREAL, HOLDRUM
2. "DEN LILLE AULA"
3. SFO
4. VÆRKSTEDSBYGNING
5. "DEN STORE AULA"
6. SKOLEKØKKEN
7. FREMTIDIG BYGGEFELT FOR KLUB
8. ADMINISTRATION/ LÆGEKLINIK
9. SPORTSHAL
10. KUNDSKABENS HAVE
11. SOPPEBASSIN
12. RAMPE
13. DYRKNINGSHAVE
14. BOLDBANER
15. BEFÆSTET LEGE- OG OPHOLDSAREALER
16. RAMBLA

GANG/ CYKELSTI

TREKRONER ALLÉ

Architects' current portfolio. With this, the firm extends the legacy from Lauritzen's interest in science and his excellent and thoughtful school projects in Gladsaxe Municipality during the 1930s and 1940s.

An educational milestone on par with the introduction of the Danish folk high school and Bauhaus: the first Summerhill School (1921) in Leiston, Suffolk.

A small school in a big world

'It was probably the vaguest programme I have ever read',[93] says architect and partner Torsten Stephensen from Vilhelm Lauritzen Architects of the architecture competition for Trekroner Skole, built in 2005 outside the city of Roskilde. The vague brief was a deliberate choice. The client, Roskilde Municipality and the Ministry of Education, wanted the architects to rethink the physical school. Stephensen sat down and revisited the school of his own childhood in his mind: a large building with long corridors, smelling of soft soap, and cramped classrooms where the pupils spent most of the day inside. Not a cheerful memory.

However, a look at the hundred-year history of Vilhelm Lauritzen Architects reveals one of the most inspiring concepts for a different kind of school architecture. Even if it was probably, in every sense of the word, in a minority category, it had considerable influence on the modern project. In Danish, the type was described as a 'little school' or 'free school'. Both qualities are essential, even if the small, free schools in Denmark and elsewhere differ widely and represent a diverse range of initiatives.

In 1924, the Scottish educator Alexander Sutherland Neill founded a school that could, with some justification, be characterized as the school of the modern project. It was called Summerhill and still exists today, in Leiston, England. To many, the school's name, with its warm connotations of happy childhood memories, represents a beacon of hope for modern education both because of the example it set and because of Neill's own advocacy work and the book[94] he wrote about the school. The goal at Summerhill was to raise children for happiness, nothing less. 'I would rather see a school produce a happy street cleaner than a neurotic scholar', Neill wrote. And even if that may sound like the very recipe for what is now associated with soft-headed hippie ideas and failure of responsibility, the implied underlying respect for the rights of the child and education without authoritarianism and disciplining have, in fact, since become the norm. At Summerhill, allowing children autonomy, as long as nobody is hurt, did not mean sheltering them but, on the contrary, giving them the freedom to develop into independent human beings.

In light of modern educational ideas, architects have of course explored how the physical school environment can promote self-development, learning experiences, safety, participatory democracy and so forth. If good architecture can create better human beings, school architecture seems an ideal place to start. In this spirit, Vilhelm Lauritzen Architects took up the client's invitation to adopt an approach that was as free and unorthodox as 'radical' education.

Architecture on a child's scale: Trekroner Skole.

'So in Trekroner we moved the corridors into the schoolyard.'

'If we get rid of the corridors, we can add 15 square metres to each classroom',[95] Torsten Stephensen reasoned. He went to inspect the site for the new school. It was located on a windswept hill in an open area with few other structures around, apart from a regional train station letting passengers off into nowhere. In the distance, the low buildings of Roskilde University nestled into the terrain. Standing here and recalling the large schools that appeared so huge and scary from a child's point of view, Stephensen intuitively thought, 'We need to build something that protects the kids',[96] he says.

The detail plan for the area was in fact quite visionary. The planners had resolved that a well-functioning residential area had to have a good school, a preschool, a shopping centre and so forth. They had also turned the housing construction process upside down:

'Instead of the municipality, a social housing association or a private investor defining and building houses that people could then choose to move into, [...] the planners attempted to have potential new residents define what type of housing they wanted to move into. Groups and associations of prospective residents were formed, and the plans for the new developments successively developed in a dialogue within the individual groups and with consultants and the municipality.'[97] The residents were on the way, including school-age children.

If a detail plan can be turned on its head, it is also possible to rethink architecture for children. For the youngest pupils in particular, it can feel overwhelming to come to a big school with many older children. Vilhelm Lauritzen Architects wanted to design 'a little school in the big school'. The youngest pupils would have their own little hall and a courtyard with fruit trees, a 'garden of knowledge' where some of the classes might be held when the weather permitted. That would also provide a space for them to be physically active and burn up some energy. In Torsten Stephensen's childhood school, running was not allowed in the corridors. 'So in Trekroner we moved the corridors into the schoolyard',[98] as he explained.

The big school of equality

Today, free schools are a common phenomenon, having grown out of Summerhill and other modern reform education initiatives. In Denmark, the first such school, Den Lille Skole (the Little School), opened in Lyngby as early as 1949. These primary and lower secondary free schools comply with the general legislation on schools and represent a wide diversity of religious, ethnic and philosophical backgrounds. Today, there are more than 500 free schools in Denmark alone and countless more throughout the world. Many are based on a particular idea or educational approach, and from the outset architecture has played a key role in maintaining the human scale – more specifically, a child's scale. With inspiration from the old village schools, free schools had to be small. But why had the ordinary schools grown so large?

With modernity came greater equality. The second word in the original credo of the Enlightenment, as was articulated during the French Revolution, is 'equality'. Thus, equality follows immediately after freedom. Both the Swiss-French philosopher Jean-Jacques Rousseau's idea that we can only achieve natural freedom in an egalitarian society and Kant's acknowledgement that freedom presupposes that everyone attain their majority treat freedom and equality as mutually dependent concepts. It is important to note there that 'equal' does not mean 'alike'.

Nature's variation is one of its main strengths, and this includes human diversity. We are as different in nature as we should be equal under the law. However, the more unequal society is the less benefit the underprivileged have from being born equal. Thus, the strongest driver of social change throughout history seems to have been the attempt of the less privileged to eliminate the structures that keep the power in the hand of the privileged classes – often by attempting to eliminate the privileged persons themselves. Which is why a revolution is not a tea party, as Mao observed.

The modern welfare society would not have been possible without greater equality, including greater equality between urban and rural areas. A hundred years ago may seem a distant past, but as a mental time machine, young readers may consider the fact that this author's father-in-law, for example, only attended school every other day. That was the custom in rural Denmark as late as the 1940s. In order to ensure that enlightenment also reached the rural parishes, new legislation in 1937 required village schools to provide the same number of lessons as schools in towns and cities.

The new law was a thoroughly progressive piece of legislation. The then Social Liberal minister of education, Jørgen Jørgensen, even revised the preamble describing the fundamental purpose of schools. Instead of producing 'good and honest people in accordance with the teachings of evangelic Christianity' and 'useful citizens of the state',[99] schools were now required to 'promote and develop the children's talents and abilities, enhance their character and give them useful knowledge'.[100] Children were no longer considered to have a given, finite set of qualities, with the task being to turn them into adults as quickly as possible. Children now had abilities to be developed, just as adults and in all areas of life. This was a little, big revolution.

However, now that children in rural districts had to show up for school every day, the village schools were no longer big enough, so all over the country, municipalities had to expand and build new schools. After the war, when school construction picked up pace, the cost must have begun to make a real impact, and from the mid 1950s the big 'central schools' began to appear, and the municipalities were encouraged to build 'rational' architecture, which meant abandoning the brick-built structures in favour of prefab concrete. In just 20 years, from 1951 to 1971, the number of municipal primary and lower secondary schools shrunk from 3,652 to 2,108.

To illustrate this trend with a glimpse of my own school experience: just as I was about to begin Year 1 in 1968, the village school two minutes up the hill from our house closed down, and I had to board the school bus to attend the central school four kilometres away.

The time of the large schools had come. And thus, in response, the time of the smaller free schools.

Modern sweeping lines in
the lobby of Kaj Gottlob's
Skolen ved Sundet and Vilhelm
Lauritzen's Marielyst Skole.
Both from 1938.

The 'aula school' and the garden of knowledge

The design of Trekroner Skole draws inspiration from the modern so-called aula school, which emerged in the mid 1920s: a school constructed around a large main hall. With tall ceilings in the central hall, long, sweeping interior galleries and tall window sections, schools such as architect Kaj Gottlob's Skolen ved Sundet (School on the Strait) were clear exponents of the modern principle of light, air and cleanliness. Vilhelm Lauritzen's Marielyst Skole (1938) in Gladsaxe was also an aula school, and as a very modern feature, all the classrooms have doors leading to the hall, which thus served both as a communal recreational space, a daily circulation space and an assembly hall for school events. Lauritzen was also early in including outdoor classes, in his design of Stengård Skole, which as mentioned earlier was built in 1952 but was designed during the war. Each classroom has access to the gardens around the low, wide buildings with pitched roofs, which are placed in a staggered formation, not unlike the detached single-family houses in the surrounding suburban neighbourhood.

Trekroner Skole consists of buildings constructed around a central quad with large high-ceilinged project rooms called 'home areas', which replace the traditional structure of classrooms along a corridor. Additional classrooms, after-school settings and so on are located in the middle. The home areas for the youngest students are placed at ground level with direct access to the outdoor areas. The 'garden of knowledge' in the middle of the complex acts as a full-scale laboratory for science, home economics and other topics. The pupils can grow their own herbs, harvest fruit from bushes and trees, follow the changing seasons, play and learn while getting plenty of fresh air.

The low buildings, which are built of large, light-coloured bricks, have many stepless entrances and are level with the outdoor areas. Their expression is simple and frank, almost as if the school had been built by a group of active, enthusiastic parents who founded their own school – the way many of the free schools were actually built. It is a municipal school with a close community feel.

Émile as a child

Gardens of knowledge as a setting for free thinking and learning have been established several times in the history of Western culture. During antiquity, the Greek philosopher Epicurus taught his students in a garden in Athens, and like his materialist nuclear theory, his thoughts on how objective sensory experience presupposes a free, unbiased approach and results in ethically appropriate actions

194

appear rather modern. The Epicurean idea that well-being could be achieved by living right, both physiologically and ethically, resonates well with modern holistic views, born out by neuroscience, which seem to be replacing the centuries-old dogma of the duality of body and soul.

The most influential – and provoking – theory of outdoor education is the one presented by Rousseau in *Émile, or On Education*, a novel, or intellectual experiment, concerning the boy Émile, who is raised in a garden, where he is protected from the harmful influences of society. In modern civilization, so the author, a person is trained 'like a saddle-horse', and children are robbed of their childhood in order to become adults as quickly as possible, which means thinking like everyone else and accepting being guided by 'prejudice, authority, necessity, example, all the social conditions into which we are plunged', says Rousseau. Instead, the 'wall' that Rousseau encourages any 'tender, anxious mother' to build around her 'child's soul'[101] should serve, above all, to protect freedom, independence and critical thinking – not only in the child but universally, lest the bad habits that come with civilization swallow up freedom of thought and lifestyle. As Rousseau writes: 'The real object of our study is man and his environment.'[102]

The study of the human environment is the necessary basis for understanding the extent to which this environment is man-made. It is up to us to define what is necessary. In the modern project, the notion that we do not need to wait for God but are capable of building the good life for ourselves here on earth is based on the conviction that society is an experiment. And that the goal is utopian – which is not to say that it is impossible.

Trekroner Skole is a reinterpretation of the traditional Danish school. There are no corridors, and the large classrooms are flooded with daylight. The central school garden, called the 'garden of knowledge', is an important learning environment that all the classrooms have direct access to.

... and as an adult

However, experiments require someone to step beyond the familiar boundaries and ask for *das ganz Andere*[103]. As Rousseau did. Or as did one of the key sources of inspiration for the environmental awareness and the reinterpretation of the modern project, American self-taught philosopher Henry David Thoreau, whose book *Walden* has also been dubbed 'Émile grown up'.[104] On a day in March, 1845, the author borrowed an axe and moved from his hometown of Concord in Massachusetts, USA, to the forest by Walden Pond, where he planned to build a cabin and figure out what is *actually* necessary. Like Rousseau's book, Thoreau's report from life in the woods is, above all, a study of man's environment and conditions and a critique of those aspects of modern civilization that we take for granted. His analysis is as incisive as the ones delivered by his contemporaries Karl Marx and Søren Kierkegaard, each from their particular perspective.

Thoreau saw the farmers toiling in their fields, day in, day out, always pushing life ahead of them so that they would never catch up until their death: 'Who made them serfs of the soil? Why should

Following spread: The Niels Bohr Building (2022) in Copenhagen. The architecture of the molecule, human curiosity and constant experimentation are reflected in the characteristic glass facade, which consists of 2,500 pyramidal pixels. In collaboration with Per Hedegaard, professor of mathematics at the University of Copenhagen, the pixel shape has been translated into the numerical system, and the pixels are mounted so that each facade encodes a famous scientific formula, including the golden section, pi, an insulin string, Hubble's law and the law of gravitation.

they eat their sixty acres, when man is condemned to eat only his peck of dirt? Why should they begin digging their graves as soon as they are born?'[105]

He observed our busy lives and our widespread, disgruntled dissatisfaction and concluded that we appear to be imposing this destiny upon ourselves, based on equally self-imposed notions of necessity: 'The mass of men lead lives of quiet desperation. What is called resignation is confirmed desperation.'[106]

Life is an experiment that we are afraid to conduct, and while 'civilization has been improving our houses, it has not equally improved the men who are to inhabit them', Thoreau observes.[107]

So he became an architect of life and moved temporarily to the edge of our civilization, albeit not so far out that he could not still follow the life we lead. He shared the findings of his experiment with us, since civilization and society are our inescapable community, and the process is irreversible, like life itself: 'I went to the woods because I wished to live deliberately, to front only the essential facts of life, and see if I could not learn what it had to teach, and not, when I came to die, discover that I had not lived.'[108]

A temple to experimentation

Designing an entire building for experiments cannot have been an easy task. Physics experiments invariably involve explosions, and laboratories have to be built to take a beating. For example, an average of one fire a week was included as a standard condition in the programme for the Niels Bohr Building designed by Vilhelm Lauritzen Architects in collaboration with architects Christensen & Co Architects, which, despite a number of challenges, is scheduled to be handed over in 2022. Another challenge is that, as mentioned earlier, functionalist architecture should express its function. If the function is experimentation, the setting has to play along, perhaps by offering a counterpoint of solid familiarity but certainly with an expression with a functional reference.

On a site outside Kongens Lyngby, Vilhelm Lauritzen Architects designed a building for the Novo Nordisk Foundation (completed in 2021) for the foundation's educational project LIFE, which aims to boost Danish schoolchildren's interest in the natural sciences.

In a sense, the building is a standard modern, rectangular glass box with two tall floors. However, the roof appears to be supported by a structure of columns that has been pulled outwards from the building, forming a frame that provides shade and filters the light, evoking the image of an ancient Greek temple. Unlike their Greek counterparts, however, the slender columns are completely straight and without capitals, fluting or any other ornamentation. Fitted with a small post base, from a distance they appear to float above the ground. The columns are placed in an asymmetrical formation with varying gaps, which one can spend a long time trying to figure out.

The temple of experimentation, LIFE Campus (2021), in Kongens Lyngby outside Copenhagen. Each of the 96 columns are 9 metres tall and made of heartwood from 150-year-old oak trees. The columns are positioned to refer to the mathematical Fibonacci sequence and to DNA strings.

Life is an experiment that we are afraid to conduct.

At the entrance to the LIFE Campus, the columns open up in a fan shape to welcome visitors.

Outdoor space designed to set the mind free among the tall grass. An 'experience path' connects the building to the landscape and guides visitors to science-inspired works by artist Jeppe Hein. The south end is home to the learning gardens LIFE Arboretum and LIFE Orchard, which feature a wide selection of trees. There are plans to establish shelters where school groups can spend the night. Landscape architecture by LYTT Architecture.

According to architect and partner at Vilhelm Lauritzen Architects Thomas West Jensen, the pattern is based on the Fibonacci sequence and other mathematical systems.

Above the main entrance to the building, which is placed in one corner, the columns are raised completely above the ground, pushed up as if a giant has squeezed in under them in an attempt to enter the building. Finally, the columns are not made of marble, stone or concrete but of light-coloured timber with the same warm glow as a Danish furniture classic. Inside, the column motif is repeated in the foyer and stairway, where the material produces the same softening contrast to the concrete floors and large glazed surfaces. The building has a footprint of just 52 by 52 metres, and this relatively small 'jewellery box' of a modern temple is located on an open meadow with tall grass in Dyrehaven, the deer park north of Copenhagen.

In the modern project, the natural sciences have taken the place of religion because they offer plausible explanations to many of the mysteries of life and nature that faith and superstition previously provided their own dubious answers to. 'Dubious' because they could not be verified outside the inherent logic of the explanations, or rather stories. In a pre-scientific age without an enlightened population, there was little need for proper verifiability, and it probably suited the small powerful elite just fine that the stories never questioned *their* role.

The unfinished house

However, the somewhat simplistic analogy of the science auditorium as the modern temple of truth is not the right comparison for the building in Kongens Lyngby. Not least because the purpose of the building reveals the continued need to preach the gospel of science to ensure the influx of new scientists and engineers. No, the beauty of the LIFE building is its scientifically *inspired*, free, inventor-like treatment of classical and modern features in a contemporary interpretation of Nordic functionalism. Gunnar Asplund, the architect of Skogskapellet, would have appreciated this building, but the main point is that the rest of us also appreciate it. We are pulled in, as if by an art installation or a puzzle, eager to crack the code. The spindly structure, the use of timber instead of concrete, and the meadow setting are subtly alluring. Symmetry and strict order would have been as out of place here as futuristic symbolism or a cool, sciency screen facing the outside world. The construction even has an unfinished feel – is that possible?

Can architecture show a sense of humour? Apparently, yes. Here, however, the humour is as far from noisy Disneyesque postmodernism as one can imagine. Rather than a shallow laugh, it calls for a thoughtful smile, as one is reminded that play and freedom are each other's conditions. What is fascinating about science is how it demonstrates that we should never stop playing, as long as we live,

Above the main entrance to the building, which is placed in one corner, the columns are raised completely above the ground, pushed up as if a giant has squeezed in under them in an attempt to enter the building.

even when it comes to serious issues such as time and space, black holes, DNA and orders of columns.

In the LIFE building Vilhelm Lauritzen Architects plays with the oldest architectural element in the world in a way that seems to merge the image of the tree trunk and the Dorian column. The effect is similar to sailing at night, when foreshortening makes two lighthouses that are in fact several nautical miles apart suddenly appear to line up – one under the other, like traffic lights – and thus sailors know they are on the right course. The free, atonal rhythms of the boxy timber colonnade give an impression of experimentation, trial and error. The building is unfinished, will never be finished, just as nature's infinite depth of mysteries will always provide more topics to study. Academic freedom implies the obligation to keep playing, whatever the rest of the world might be focused on, until the truth suddenly appears like a flash at the base of the test tube.

It is this freedom that the LIFE structure offers the schoolchildren who cross the grassy meadow to this temple of experimentation. It appears to meet this requirement by simple means and with playful ease, but in fact the solution is the result of a lengthy architectural experiment, which includes motifs from antiquity, Gothic methods, some Mannerism, a good dose of Nordic neoclassicism, modernism and postmodernism and, finally, contemporary global contextualism. That may sound like an explosive mix, but no worries, there are concrete columns inside the building. The expression is far from dully didactic but rather exemplary in the sense that the architects are demonstrating how serious they are when they play. Theory can be desperately dull, including the theory of aesthetics. However, when it all adds up, the result is exhilarating, like the beauty of a mathematical equation.

If the straight path from school to research and Nobel Prizes may seem a bit of a strain at times, with the LIFE building the architects have successfully demonstrated, in their own medium, how fast time moves along the section one has measured out once the experimenter boards the mystery. The brief was not to build an auditorium or a laboratory or a classroom. Of course it was that too, but above all the brief called for a building that illustrates what serious play is. A building that fulfils its function by containing a mystery in itself. They built it in a way that exemplifies functionalism. Nothing less.

Vilhelm Lauritzen Architects is functionalist in its approach in precisely that sense. 'The form is an imprint of what happens inside the building', as partner Anne Møller Sørensen puts it. 'Above all, our architecture should be meaningful to the users. As keen as we are to explore new territory, we place an equal priority on function and needs. We don't necessarily see a conflict between creating innovative architecture and creating architecture that is site-specific, timeless and durable.'

All research begins with wondering. 'Floating' columns frame the entrance to the LIFE Campus.

Among the settings for learning are four professional laboratories, where children and young people can work on the same current challenges facing society that researchers are working on in companies and universities.

202

The corner is the display

As another architect and partner at Vilhelm Lauritzen Architects, Simon Natanael Svensson, observes: 'Sometimes, good architecture is architecture you don't notice.'[109]

That the best architecture might be architecture that simply works, without anyone noticing it or being able to say exactly why it works so well, suggests why functionalism in modern architecture has survived changing fashions. It also explains why the term 'functionalism' may be the best definition of the aesthetic of modern architecture, beyond any discussions about geometric versus organic shapes, pared-down expressions versus a more exuberant, ornamented style and so forth. The deliberate understatement or resource efficiency in 'making the most out of minimalism',[110] as Simon Natanael Svensson puts it, has proven to be a durable strategy across countless structural changes in society and in the construction industry and across changing fashions and trends that influence clients and decision makers.

This is more easily said than done, however. Not least at what is probably the best-known and busiest corner in Denmark: the location of the department store Illum (2016) on Amagertorv near the Stork Fountain in the middle of the pedestrian street Strøget in central Copenhagen. As with the LIFE building near the deer park, this building too makes its purpose clear from a distance. In a renovation of this highly visible location, Vilhelm Lauritzen Architects created an accentuation that is meaningful to the users – in this case, everyone who passes by.

The windows of the four floors above the street level now appear as something in between display cases and shop windows in varying sizes. This makes passers-by raise their gaze, so that, for once, they see something other than just the street-level shop displays.

The display cases have differing widths and heights, and some of them wrap around the corners, while others do not. Similarly, the bronze-anodized frames on a calm background of light-coloured sandstone have different depths. The varying depths and formats produce a fascinating play of light and shade throughout the day. Even if the specific products might not hold an appeal, the building itself offers an interesting display: a lively mosaic that reflects the constant bustle of people on the square and in the two pedestrian streets that come together here, movements that the mannequins in the display cases capture for a moment in their frozen ballet. The window niches point back in time and further down the street to the closed panels in the same colour and material, which have defined Illum's facade since the 1970s.

The corner towards the Stork Fountain is part of a larger refurbishment of the department store aiming to revitalize this element in the particular urban character of Copenhagen's historical city centre. The project adds something new in order to highlight qualities in the existing building. Attention is directed towards the details by means of a few distinctive features that produce a high degree of variation. In this way, each detail takes on greater significance. By deviating from the serial repetition of identical elements, the architecture introduces a tiny disruption, as the irregularities of hand-crafted features once did, an effect that can still be pursued through controlled ageing and patination.

In the refurbishment, the long facades towards Strøget and Pilestræde were vertically segmented in an expression resembling

A corner that is neither round nor sharp. In a clear, original expression, the Illum corner with its simple relief structure engages in a modern interplay with the older, ornamented buildings nearby.

Illum (2016) on the corner Købmagergade and Strøget in Copenhagen is a reinterpretation of a modern classic: the shop window. The building is clad in light-coloured sandstone with anodized bronze window frames.

In a clearing near Esrum Lake on the edge of the woods lie 20 student dwellings from 2019 that are part of the Forest and Landscape College. The college was founded in 1948 in order to give foresters new skills and knowledge. Today, it is part of the University of Copenhagen and offers training in natural and cultural heritage management or forestry and landscape engineering.

Brick relief on the European School Copenhagen (2018) in Carlsberg Byen in Copenhagen.

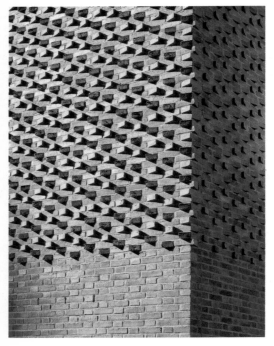

smaller townhouses. With a more clearly defined base and roof, they now blend more smoothly in among the surrounding 19th-century buildings. In this way, a modern building has been elegantly adapted to the streetscape with a minimalist intervention.

In the middle of the forest

With the student housing for the Forest and Landscape College (2019) in Nødebo in northern Zealand, Vilhelm Lauritzen Architects built something almost as unostentatious as Thoreau's cabin in the woods.

The tall, plain, long building with two floors is clad with a syncopated pattern of narrow timber battens painted black, the roof covered with black roofing felt. Light apertures with white window frames are asymmetrically distributed to match the building's interior layout rather than a rigid facade concept. At one end of the building, an exterior stair to the upper floor is pulled in, sheltered by the building and half concealed behind the facade. At the opposite end, the south-facing end wall has been opened to accommodate a covered balcony on top and a patio below. Deciduous trees stand close around the building and are reflected in the window panes, while the forest floor continues all the way up to the structure.

The student housing is in close visual communication with the college buildings, which consist of a former farmhouse with later, separate extensions in a similarly understated modern forest cabin style. The students are training in natural and cultural heritage management or forestry and landscape engineering, among other subjects, at the University of Copenhagen. The building is designed to accommodate their everyday needs, which calls for slightly different practical solutions than standard student housing: by the main entrance there is a mud room with an outdoor tap, so they can pull off dirty outerwear and boots before coming inside. In every way, this is a sturdy building, capable of standing up to wear and tear throughout the year in the middle of a forest.

In the middle of the city

If we replace forest with city and the beech trees of Gribskov forest with the red brickwork of Carlsberg Byen (Carlsberg City), then the programme for the European School Copenhagen (2018), co-designed

A home in the woods that serves also as a university and learning space. The building is designed to have a discreet and respectful presence in nature.

The European School
Copenhagen has 900 students
and fits into the historical
setting on a plot that is no
bigger than four average plots
for single-family houses. To
make up for the small footprint,
the school makes use of the
vertical dimension, here with an
elevated playground on a first-
storey level, where everyone is
welcome outside school hours.

*Whether Vitruvius during
antiquity, Alberti during the
Renaissance or Ruskin
during the Romantic era or
all the other architecture
theorists, none of them dealt
with architecture and space.*

with NORD Architects, is a perfect parallel to the forest project. The plot is fairly small, just 4,700 square metres, and the brief called for a 14,000-square-metre 'modern learning environment'[111] for 900 students and designed to match the atmospheric, dense Carlsberg area with its preservation-worthy elements of cultural and industrial history. The solution was a five-storey perimeter block in red brick – as the familiar, well-aged, Copenhagen buildings but varied in construction and details – cut off and opened up to form an urban space in combination with the school's gym, in a separate building. In some sections of the exterior wall, the bricks are tilted to form a relief effect that relates to the ornamentation of the existing buildings.

The plot is located between Ny Carlsberg Vej and the new square Franciska Clausens Plads, which emerged as a result of the design. The new square has added a third dimension to the urban space, because it continues at street level into the school canteen as well as up the stairs onto the roof of the canteen, where it creates a schoolyard, slightly sheltered but still in close contact with the city. Just as the gym may be experienced as a covered continuation of the square, the block with its long, flat stairs and playfully varied composed light apertures reaches into the urban space that the square forms.

Long balcony lines showing the way in Pier E at Copenhagen Airport.

The space of architecture

Whether the site is an open field, a clearing in the wood or a plot in the heart of the city, it is characteristic of Vilhelm Lauritzen Architects that the point and the effect of their buildings have more to do with the space they create than with the walls that define them. For example, Copenhagen Business School in Frederiksberg – like DR Byen, Pier E in Copenhagen Airport and the Novozymes building in Lyngby and many other major contemporary projects – is organized around interior 'streets'. As the term suggests, the interior street has the dual purpose of transferring the qualities of the urban space to the interior of the building and simultaneously extending the spatial qualities of the building beyond the structure itself, for example through measures that soften the transition between indoors and out. This spatial focus is not unique to Vilhelm Lauritzen Architects, neither in a contemporary context nor in modern architecture at large. If one were to ask any architect what the principal task of architecture is, he or she would be likely to say 'to create spaces'.

That is new. Or rather, it is modern. In almost two thousand years of reflections on the potential and requirements of architecture, the word 'space' does not occur. Whether Vitruvius during antiquity, Alberti during the Renaissance or Ruskin during the Romantic era or all the other architecture theorists, none of them dealt with architecture and space. For example, if we compare a plan drawing of Brunelleschi's Santo Spirito church in Florence from 1487 with a plan of Le Corbusier's Carpenter Center at Harvard University from 1963, it is clear that the relationship between the two phenomena

To the left, a plan of Brunelleschi's Santo Spirito Church (1487) in Florence; to the right, a plan of Le Corbusier's Carpenter Center (1963) at Harvard University.

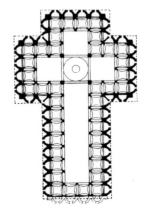
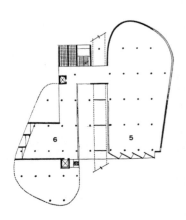

An almost classically light and musical facade composition. Notice the harlequin pattern in the lively frieze that is repeated in a different variant inside on the balcony.

Facade pause. The beautifully handled transition between two materials, two buildings, two architectural periods. The People's House and its neighbour on Enghavevej in Copenhagen.

Carefully considered facade detailing in apparent simplicity.

of *space* and *wall* changed dramatically during architecture history. While Brunelleschi's plan shows walls and columns that define where the space emerges, Le Corbusier's plan shows spaces that determine where the walls go. An inverse perspective.

In recent years, this transformation has enabled a huge liberation of the physical conditions of architecture, not unlike the weightless and wirelessness of modern life. With the latest new construction methods and computer design, the old architectural dream of creating wide spans boldly floating ever farther away from necessity – the load-bearing structures – has become possible, enabling architects to stretch, twist and mould shapes, causing familiar terms such as wall, facade and roof to lose much of their meaning. The downside is that it takes strong professional discipline and artistic moderation not to go mad in formalism and quirky ideas. However, the upside far outweighs this risk: we can now consider our interaction with our physical environment at a much deeper level and with much greater freedom, new concepts are easy to test, and the experiments can inspire subsequent analyses.

Vilhelm Lauritzen Architects' own description of the European School Copenhagen reflects the awareness that the liberation of architectural space must benefit everyone:

'The building was designed as a school that offers rich experiences, where the historical surroundings stimulate and inspire play and learning. The many passages and the smooth transitions between the school and the public space contribute to a dynamic urban space on a human scale. At the same time, the building adds value for the whole district, because its areas are open to everyone.'[112]

The abstract quality keeps the door open

The street inside the building and the covered urban space may be popular right now, but they are probably as old as architecture itself. Their equivalents are found in the temples of antiquity, with their halls supported by columns and their colonnades, and in the loggia in Mediterranean architecture, which for centuries has been so widely copied. A modern loggia is found just a stone's throw from the European School Copenhagen. On Enghavevej, between 1953 and 1956, Vilhelm Lauritzen created a place that would contain, enlighten and entertain the community: the People's House, which is now the concert venue VEGA. Quite in line with the fundamental principles of functionalism, the covered colonnade serves the practical purpose of keeping concert-goers dry on rainy nights as they wait for the doors to open. The building, which was originally built for Arbejdernes Fællesorganisation (the Federation of Workers) and has hosted thousands of concerts since 1996, remains modern in both function and expression.

209

Contemporary shopping centres are also modelled on the *passage* of early modernity, the glazed-in shopping arcade which cuts through Parisian city blocks. Like the tall, arched, glazed-in platforms of the railway stations and the botanical gardens' tropical greenhouses, these passages are examples of the larger interior space that was made possible by modern industrialized construction techniques. As mentioned earlier, until the 19th century it had not been possible to produce steel and glass in sufficiently large dimensions to be used in construction, but with new glass-making methods, steel girders and the invention of reinforced concrete, it became easier to construct larger spans and possible to do it on an industrial scale.

The aesthetic of modern architecture is a good example of the interaction that commonly arises between new technology and design. The steel girders made it possible to release the building facades from their structural load-bearing role, and architects used this freedom to create much thinner glass facades, which in turn led to an expression that increased the popularity of this construction method further. The same is true of the strength and form potential of reinforced concrete, which allowed for buildings that looked like sculptures, for example based on the ocean liner's rounded, streamlined shapes, which are common in modern architecture.

Similarly spatial functions apply to interior atriums, stairwells with room for socializing, courtyards between buildings, rooftop patios and other architectural elements that characterize contemporary architecture. Like indoors and outdoors, they are often only separated by glass or brickwork, which seems to be without significance for the building's construction and often extends into the surrounding landscape as free-standing structures. Characteristic of modern, spatially oriented architectural design, contemporary architects often describe the building's facades, floors and so forth as 'slices': abstract building blocks whose material character, constructive and spatial function and ultimate design remain open and 'in suspension' as long as possible in the design process.

Architects constantly have to imagine what does not exist yet, and the spatial perception of modern design surely has not made that task any easier. It must be harder to deal with slices in an empty space than with a symmetrical facade composed on a traditional builder's recipe of 'pillar – window – pillar – window – pillar – main door / pillar – window – pillar – window –pillar – downpipe'. However, like space in modern visual art, where everything seems to be free-floating, overlapping and transparent, as if we were looking at atoms before they pull together into solid form, modern architecture's empty space can also be perceived as freedom. And perhaps modern architecture's most important contribution to the modern project is the fact that its spatial intangibility reminds us of infinite possibility: 'And what is empty turns its face to us and whispers: "I am not empty, I am open"', as the Swedish poet Tomas Tranströmer writes.[113]

Simple organic shapes and lines with both the two VEGA Chairs Lauritzen designed for the building, one of which has now gone back into production.

One of Lauritzen's lamps lights up a teak panel with the characteristic combination of diffuse and directional lighting.

Warm, golden notes and black-and-white contrasting patterns. Everything matches and is carefully incorporated into the whole, even the emergency exit sign.

Following spread: The large hall at the People's House (1956). The room can be expanded or closed off as needed.

211

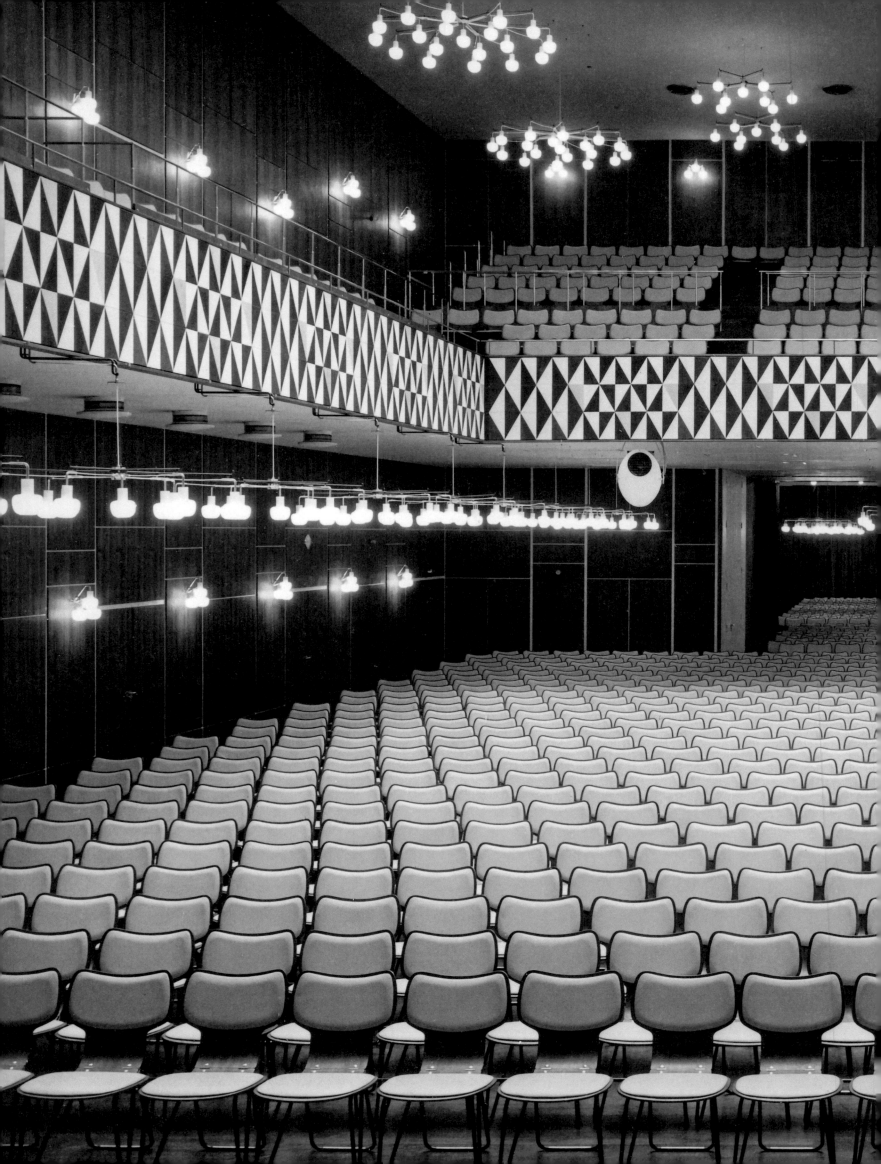

6

The necessary finesse

The purpose of minimalism

The aesthetic of modern architecture is so distinctive that it has often stood in the way of the modern project as a whole: clean lines and white surfaces, shiny steel and large panes of glass, half-empty rooms with furniture spaced far apart, openness, visible constructions, the expression pared down to a narrow range of elements and shapes and a minimal use of materials. This minimalism almost gives the impression that the aesthetic of modern architecture has an inherent moral. The aesthetic is in fact an ethos; its credo is 'less is more'.

Like welfare architecture and functionalism, this minimalism has helped keep the modern project alive for more than a hundred years – as a style in virtually all art forms, fashion, home interiors and so forth and, most recently, as an environmentally aware and climate-conscious lifestyle among Western youth, who are

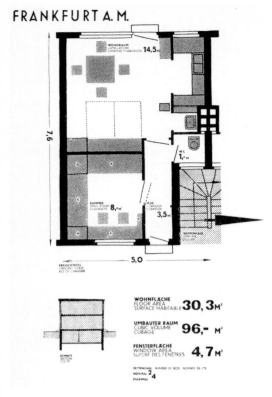

FRANKFURT A.M.

WOHNFLÄCHE
FLOOR AREA
SURFACE HABITABLE **30,3** M²

UMBAUTER RAUM
CUBIC VOLUME
CUBAGE **96,-** M³

FENSTERFLÄCHE
WINDOW AREA
SUPERF DES FENETRES **4,7** M²

Functionalism as a focus on necessity. Proposal for floor plan for a flat. Illustration from the catalogue for the second CIAM exhibition, 'Minimum Dwelling', at Haus Werkbund in Frankfurt am Main, 1929. Note the space-saving bed that pops out of the closet.

rediscovering earlier subcultures and shaping their own, which may gain very widespread traction thanks to globalization and social media.

On the other hand, this tendency for moralizing maxims and a spartan style may in fact be one of the biggest problems of the modern aesthetic. Certainly, as early as 1939, the first historian of modern architecture, Sigfried Giedion, argued that the growing criticism of modern architecture stemmed from its apparent disregard for beauty and emotions in architectural expression in favour of an exclusive focus on the necessity of serving the 'strictly functional'. That was a dead end, according to Giedion, who called on architects to meet our inescapable desire for luxury in a 'legitimate and vital way'.[114]

This call lies in direct extension of the famous concept of the Minimum Dwelling, the theme of the internationally oriented architecture event CIAM[115] in Frankfurt in 1929 – where Giedion was among the participants. Minimum may sound a bit sparse, but if the concept is seen in light of the modern urge for rational, scientifically inspired analysis of all phenomena in their smallest components and the critical Rousseauian 'study of man and his environment', it becomes easier to understand why the modern project is taking such an interest in minimalism.

That less may well be more than much is an aesthetic experience that is aligned with a similar ethical or general existential experience: the exquisite is worth more than the watered down, and a more focused approach is almost always superior. In the complex and often costly endeavour of architecture, as with fighter jets or film productions, a thoughtful use of resources is essential. This thoughtfulness quickly becomes a good habit.

The high architectural standard that Vilhelm Lauritzen Architects and colleagues have attained over the past hundred years and which we have begun to take for granted, at least in a contemporary Danish and Nordic context, springs from an ambitious professional aesthetic-ethical approach that involves thorough analysis of needs, environment, economics, spatial and constructive potentials and many other aspects. Much of the time, this is addressed in a communication process in close collaboration with the client, users and other professions involved in construction. Today, the exquisite is a combination of good details such as functionality, economy, sustainability, user involvement, honesty, sensuous qualities and durability, which, importantly, must be 'democratic' – that is, widely available. A luxury for the many.

When this is accomplished, a modern 'minimalist' aesthetic is not a detractor from the project overall. On the contrary, it expresses what might be called the necessary finesse. The architecture firm is a key contributor in this 'basic research' into the modern aesthetic. By virtue of the tradition that is the firm's legacy, Vilhelm Lauritzen Architects may even have a particular obligation to help develop and update this aesthetic for the 21st century. An update that will bring it safely through the next hundred years.

The buildings in the Punkthusene development have a clear internal architectural relationship. By extending the penthouse floors past the edge of the roofs and similarly extending the bases past the exterior walls of the buildings, the architects have achieved a powerful expression and also allowed for rooftop patios on several levels.

With their rounded forms, the buildings are compact, well-shaped, attractive and cool, like an Apple product; they make you want to pick them up or keep them in your pocket, like a pebble found on the beach.

Each building is structured around a central core. That made it possible to design the white and blue facades without vertical elements, in a clear reference to the waves of Øresund.

The independent building

Almost on the border between Copenhagen and Hellerup, on the coast road Strandvejen, lie three buildings that seem to be too small to be office buildings or housing blocks and too big to be single-family houses. They look more like modern palaces, modelled on the urban or winter residences of royals and nobility, a type named after the Roman emperors' residences on Rome's Palatine Hill but with elements dating all the way back to the Pharaohs in Egypt and the Ming Dynasty in China. And that is indeed what they are, even if the terminology of modern architecture uses the more modest term 'point block'.

Vilhelm Lauritzen Architects designed the master plan for the area, called Tuborg Syd (Tuborg South) after the Tuborg breweries, which were located here for a hundred years from 1873 to the merger with Carlsberg in 1970 and the demolition of most of the plant around 2000. The firm also designed several other buildings in the area, including the building of the Royal Danish Yacht Club on the marina in Tuborg Harbour.

Each of the Punkthusene (Point Blocks) (2009) was designed to work either as a shared office space for several smaller companies or as an HQ for a larger enterprise. The three buildings are almost identical, except that the floor plans are angled slightly differently, and they are 'placed at a perfect mutual distance that simultaneously ties them together and lets them appear as independent', as the critic for the journal *Byggeri* Terkel Grum-Schwensen wrote.[116]

Even from a distance, the distinctive aesthetic expression of the Punkthusene is striking. They are instantly recognizable, and the expression is quintessentially modern. With their rounded forms, the buildings are compact, well-shaped, attractive and cool, like an Apple product; they make you want to pick them up or keep them in your pocket, like a pebble found on the beach. From afar, it does not seem possible, and on approaching, it is surprising to find that each building actually has no fewer than seven floors.

Perhaps this is because the architects have cleverly made the buildings appear less monumental and more sporty by pulling the penthouse floor back slightly from the facade, while the ground floor has been pushed out accordingly. This makes for a more dynamic expression and also makes room for rooftop patios above the ground floor and on the penthouse floor. They are constructed around a core with just four load-bearing columns. This enables open floors with ample air and daylight and workplaces with sweeping views of the canal and the Øresund strait. The critic for *Byggeri* thus found that the buildings' relatively modest size of approximately 500 square metres per floor makes the office space more intimate, noted a pleasant acoustic environment and concluded that the Punkthusene offer 'exceptional and unparalleled workspaces'.

The Punkthusene are genuinely modern in their generous spatial clarity with a Nordic 'organic' modern character stemming from the ice green, discreetly patterned, undulating facade bands of coloured glass. The decoration may be a nod to Louis Henry Sullivan, whose signature style was the decoration of otherwise clean facades with stylized vines or geometric ribbons with Celtic inspiration.

With the horizontally unbroken rows of windows, alternately covered and revealed by the undulating face bands, the distinct, rounded shapes of the buildings and their solitary but connected distribution on the plot, the buildings exude a sense of confident calm, quite unlike the stressful client branding of the energetically rising share market graphs on the facades of the neighbouring Saxo Bank.

With the formal reference to nearby Øresund, the buildings effortlessly play the part of both iceberg and Titanic, sandcastle and ship. One can almost feel a gentle rocking sensation, as if one were stretched out on an air mattress wearing sunglasses, floating on long, lazy waves, watching the sky and the drifting clouds. The striking characteristic of the Punkthusene in Tuborg South is thus how modern they are. In their open-space construction, in the way they relate to their surroundings and in their general aesthetic and 'style'.

Even the best architecture has style

In their repudiation of the parade of historical styles, the early modern architects furiously rejected the concept of style, and the word has generally been disliked among architects ever since, because it is, rightly, perceived as trivializing and categorising an architectural expression that is created in a complex working process involving programme analysis, studies of the environment and spatial affordances, technical conditions and so on.

However, one of the benefits of recent years' pragmatic approach in architecture and in culture overall is that many of the old opposing distinctions seem superfluous and impractical, a waste of time. There is nothing wrong with combining thoroughness with attitude. Having style is not necessarily the same as being superficial. Not only is it quite possible to be both intelligent and good-looking, depth and surface almost seem to mutually condition each other, since the given and the made no longer seem to be unambiguously separate either. Take artificial insemination, for example. Thus, perhaps we might once again speak of modern architecture as (also) being a style, having style, being stylish.

The mere mention of an aesthetic of modern architecture already seems to betray the idea that modern architecture, with its functionalist programme, buried aesthetics along with the history of style. However, from the outset, both the critics of modern architecture and many of its proponents, claimed that this was not the case, and that the catchy slogans and mottos that accompany any new movement, were oversimplifying matters. Architecture cannot be without style, to make an equally cut-and-dried statement. Even if we reduce architecture to its most basic definition of the organization of space, a roof over people's heads, it is still a statement, a sign, if you like, that has to be decoded in order to become architecture. Even a cave becomes architecture the moment someone decodes it as a dwelling.

Pergola shadows inspired by the work of American architect Louis Kahn. The joint embassy for Denmark, Norway and Iceland in Maputo (2000).

Rocky waves in modern architecture

Take an aesthetic feature such as the reference to green waves in the facade expression of the Punkthusene. The reference is dual, as it points both to the *context*, the waves of Øresund, and the maritime style that is a common theme in modern architecture. In the clever variation on this theme in the Punkthusene, however, it does not come across as a tired cliché or as one of the retro phenomena that have been the height of fashion in industrial design for decades. Rather, the facade expression appears as the result of obvious iconographic research.

It is an artistic device that is probably as old as architecture itself: drawing on the statement of another work of architecture by referring to a single part, *pars pro toto*, and thus symbolically, via a single motif, recreating the model's statement. We know it from church architecture, for example, where a circular nave, as in the round churches, is a reference to Jesus's grave in the round Church of the Holy Sepulchre in Jerusalem.

There are numerous maritime features in the aesthetic of modern architecture, especially in the early examples, and today there are far more ocean liners in white painted concrete or brick – complete with round porthole windows and balconies resembling the captain's bridge – docked in the city streets around the world than sail the seas. The old romantic notion of the free life of a sailor probably also played into this, and the so-called 'streamlined' look was all the rage in industrial design, architecture and fashion during the 1920s and 1930s. The shapes of the steam and diesel engine ships, in their fusion of sailing boat and locomotive, were the best expression of the dizzying newness of modernity.

Movement, unprecedented speed, instantaneous global telecommunication, the purely functional, powerful and, in every sense of the word, non-human quality of the machines, which could achieve things no human had ever been capable of since the beginning of evolution. Like 'aeronautics', which characteristically means 'the science of sailing in air', the nautical or maritime theme symbolized speed and freedom. In *Vers une architecture* Le Corbusier thus illustrated the concept of modern versus outdated with collages of pictures of streamlined luxury liners versus examples of monumental Parisian architecture such as Notre Dame and Garnier's opera house.

Letting in the sun

Vilhelm Lauritzen Architects preserves the traditional notion that the two finest expressions of modern architecture belong to separate genres. The expression of white, sculptural reinforced concrete

The pergola sends the hot air upwards and produces a pleasantly temperate space underneath, a space that is as undefinable as either indoors or outdoors as it is well-defined in its functionality and modern aesthetic.

The embassy appears as a monolith in concrete cast in situ and is divided into two independent representations with a shared building in between. Originally, one of the two symmetrical buildings represented Denmark and Iceland, while the other represented Norway. Today, the embassy is shared by Germany and Norway. It was constructed in collaboration with local builders, using local materials.

The distinctive steel pergola that forms a roof over the embassy patio was inspired by the work of Louis Kahn. The steel helps cool the patio by generating natural ventilation from warm air rising up from the floor. The white painted walls enclose the tiled patios, which are kept cool and shady by the pergola. To the east there is a view of the Indian Ocean.

is thus mainly reserved for cultural buildings and – translated into Nordic brick and timber – housing, health and education. On the other hand, the International Style in glass and steel is still primarily used for commercial architecture for companies and organizations. The distinction is not applied with perfect consistency, and perhaps it is arbitrary, since regardless of the expression, the core of the design process is typically the process of spatial organization, initiated by analyses of functionality, needs and context.

The context may be the local climate, if that presents a dominating factor, as in Vilhelm Lauritzen Architects' design of the joint embassy for Denmark, Norway and Iceland in Mozambique's capital, Maputo (2000).[117] Here, white concrete slices were used to break up the light apertures horizontally and thus catch the African sun and soften it into useable daylight before it is eased into the offices. Tinted windows would probably have had a similar effect, as measured on a thermometer. However, seen from inside, the world outside would have appeared in a dampened, unrealistically muted light, and from the street, the facade would have appeared blank and unapproachable, the very opposite of Nordic diplomacy.

With the same effect as the white sun-blocking concrete blinds, the inner courtyard between the two building volumes that make up the complex is covered by a steel pergola, inspired by a non-realized consulate building in Angola's capital, Luanda, designed by the famous and influential, especially among architects, American architect Louis Kahn. The pergola sends the hot air upwards and produces a pleasantly temperate space underneath, a space that is as undefinable as either indoors or outdoors as it is well-defined in its functionality and modern aesthetic.

Similarly, the new joint Danish and Icelandic embassy in New Delhi signals openness and democracy while also respecting and adapting to the local context. The exterior walls are light-coloured with distinctive vertical slats shading the often intense sunlight while offering views of the sky and of the small park where the embassy is located. Here too, the playful feature of exterior vertical and horizontal concrete slats makes it possible to avoid coated glass, so that the bright colours of the embassy garden form a welcoming interior environment. The vertical and horizontal slats are thus a further interpretation and development of the project in Mozambique as well as an interpretation of the northern Indian tradition for verandas with filigree screens.

In the very different climate of Ørestad, the handling of daylight matches the Nordic setting. All the administrative and editorial offices in Vilhelm Lauritzen Architects' section of DR Byen are placed on the second floor or higher, with ample influx of light. Despite – or perhaps because of – the Nordic climate, the naturally lit room in the Nordic variant of modern architecture is characterized by consistent attempts at dissolving the barrier between indoors and out. As in a Cubist painting, otherwise solid forms seem to overlap, break apart or intersect. Large glass panes and 'outdoor' materials used indoors and building sections that extend into the landscape create an illusion that becomes a dynamic reality when the glass turns out to be a sliding door, or when one steps into an atrium that acts as a funnel providing a direct connection to the sky. This sense of freedom, achieved through a reconciliation of nature with the cultural element that we add by means of the few, minimal elements making up the construction, is one of the more appealing aspects of the modern aesthetic.

DR Byen (2009) seen from outside on the canal and inside with the interior street. The building's structure continues into the landscape with an openness reminiscent of a Greek temple. In combination with the ample influx of natural light, this openness helps tie indoors and outdoors together.

The Danish and Icelandic Embassy in India (2019). The distinctive vertical and horizontal slats are designed to follow the journey of the sun across the sky, constructively providing shade from intense sunlight while still letting in light and offering views.

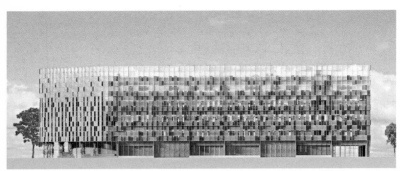

Trælasthuset (2023) in Nordhavn is clad with a pixelated relief in cork and recycled aluminium.

Architecture's dialogue with the visual arts

Parking structures are not the most cherished building types. Above-ground structures may not be as intensely disliked as underground parking structures, which due to their common role as scary locations in TV thrillers seem invariably unnerving, regardless of any soothing background music or reassuring signs announcing constant surveillance, but even parking structures above ground are rarely regarded as architecture. Open and wind-swept, in booming, raw concrete, with oil stains and their content of empty tin boxes, most of them in silver or anthracite grey, silent, their tiny red alarm diodes blinking: don't get too close, or I'll squeal!

It is also easy to see them as the ultimate testimony to the failure of urban planning in a dystopian era that surely must soon be over: imagine, towards the end, it was necessary to use precious urban land just to move the cars slightly off the street, which they had completely taken over and subjugated, while the human inhabitants had to squeeze by, pushed up against the building walls.

In other words, the parking structure as genre calls for a different approach if it is to be recognized as architecture. Vilhelm Lauritzen Architects clearly saw this task as an *artistic* challenge, which makes sense. It is often in the most obscure areas, in *terrains vagues* and in other residual products of civilization that modern art can open a crack to something different. Just as early modern architects were interested in contemporary Cubist painting and sculpture and transferred this new spatial vision to architecture, it remains a modern practice to be in close dialogue with contemporary art in the architectural design process.

In some projects this dialogue consists in a collaboration between architect and artist or craft maker, where the two interpret each other's work in a creative process that results in two independent but interrelated works: a building and its ornament or art, or where the architect leaves parts of the design to an artist or a maker who designs textiles, signage, colour scheme, interior design concept or similar aspects. In other cases, the architect uses the building facade as a canvas or turns the building into an urban art installation.

The architecture firm thus covered the parking structure Trælasthuset (Timber Warehouse) in Nordhavn with a pixelated relief in cork and recycled aluminium. Cork is a new facade material in the Nordic context but is not that uncommon in southern Europe, where cork oaks grow naturally. In addition to the many known qualities of cork as insulation and flooring, it is apparently also a sustainable solution.[118]

To be 'pixelated',[119] the facade must first be seen as an image, rather than only being perceived as a shell or an 'envelope', as architects call it. A relief is a visual medium positioned somewhere in between image, sculpture and architecture, and all facades are reliefs, but it is in the free treatment, as here, that it breaks free from the specific architectural context and becomes an independent image – only to then, in the next moment, reappear in its spatial function as part of a building with a specific function.

In architecture, it is often in building types without human inhabitants, such as the transformer station, the power station or, as here, the parking structure, that the form most conspicuously de-

Open and wind-swept, in booming, raw concrete, with oil stains and their content of empty tin boxes, most of them in silver or anthracite grey, silent, their tiny red alarm diodes blinking: don't get too close, or I'll squeal!

taches from its function and becomes an almost abstract expression. There are many architecturally interesting district heating stations in Denmark, and someone passing by one of them in a car might momentarily wonder whether they missed the unveiling of a new work by sculptor Ingvar Cronhammar, who explores and masters this delicate balance between sculpture and architecture with great finesse. Vilhelm Lauritzen Architects' Trælasthuset joins this elevated company of exotica in the Danish landscape.

Modern features that are here to stay

Which of the aesthetic attitudes of modern architecture will still be around in another hundred years?

Certainly, what might be described as the 'formal attitude'. In recent years, it has become clear that modern architecture is not as geometrically rectilinear as its reputation would have it. New construction methods and digital technology have facilitated many new forms, but even early modernism had no fear of curving lines, especially not in a Nordic context. The experimentation went as far as constructions and clients could bear. The undulating roof on Vilhelm Lauritzen's first airport building is as closely related to Aalto's door handles and Le Corbusier's chapel at Ronchamp as it is to Vilhelm Lauritzen Architects' and Herzog & de Meuron's amoeba-shaped New North Zealand Hospital. Straight lines are no more ideologically correct than curvy ones. It is the same line, and as the German-Swiss artist Paul Klee reminds us, the line is simply a formal element in a continuum from point to line to surface. On that continuum, the modern space emerges.

It is also clear that the honesty of early modern architecture when it comes to demonstrating how something is constructed has survived a hundred years and is here to stay. The same is probably true of the geometric realism that replaced symbolic ornamentation. It is all laid bare, no loose-fitting garments here; everything will be revealed anyway once it is time to appear in a bathing suit for the first time since last year's beach season. Or maybe you poke fun, exaggerate a little, turn a brick inside out or pretend the roof is patched, as on a dilapidated old hovel.

Modern architecture's open space has also definitely entered our ordinary visual vocabulary – from home to office, school, the public space and all the way round.

Finally, there is what could be called Vilhelm Lauritzen Architects' speciality, the understated aspect of the modern expression that leaves room for interpretation, for the user and so on.

The characteristic clover shape of the New North Zealand Hospital (2025).

The facade of the new parking structure Trælasthuset is a relief with a light installation, reminding us that architecture is (also) art.

Understated effects in a
room with a strictly functional
form. The metro station at
Copenhagen Airport (2007).

Understated effects

Take the metro station that the firm delivered along with their Terminal 3 for Copenhagen Airport. Strictly speaking, it is simply a glazed passage. The repetition of glazed sections on both sides of the passage creates a bright, calm space, and the long floor space is interrupted only by the escalators leading to the terminal and the car park. But then something happens. The glass comes to life, a train rolls in, and the glazed passage itself becomes a train. Almost like the effect of sitting in one train when the train on the adjacent track begins to move and for a moment it is hard to tell which train is actually moving.

Here, the architecture is so understated that it has to be wound like a music box to play its tune, and this is where its sensitivity to the given task becomes apparent. The architects clearly grasped that the simultaneously functional and formal accordance between the train and the glazed passage can be used to create a playground for the imagination, precisely where people are most bored, simply waiting. The architectural device that is so discreet it is barely there makes us see the train as a rolling glazed passage and the passage as an unmoving train. This is like a child's refreshing perspective on the potential of architecture, manifested with an adult's understated humour.

The deliberately understated or empathetic and receptive is often found in the best contemporary architecture. This may be because architecture – unlike ordinary, anonymous house construction – had traditionally been defined by the opposite qualities: the rigorously organized column-borne manifestation of the temples of antiquity, the soaring heights of Gothic cathedrals, the lavishness and monumentality of palaces and so forth. Later modern architecture certainly represents a quiet rebellion against architecture's distant elegance. Empathetic form is not just about tuning into and adapting to natural settings or about functional flexibility but contains a wide spectrum of artistic features and is constantly sprouting new, often surprising expressions. Thus also in the work of Vilhelm Lauritzen Architects.

Train pulling away from the metro station that is an extension of Terminal 3.

Recycling industrial culture

The understated or empathetic quality in Vilhelm Lauritzen Architects' practice is a good reflection of a modern grasp of the time, since an important element in contemporary architecture practice is knowing how to recycle and transform existing resources. For example the infrastructure of industrial culture.

Just when the industrial culture of the modern era was taking root in the traditionally agricultural nation of Denmark, it was losing its role as the structure underpinning society. From the early 1960s, the number of industrial jobs began to decrease, and Denmark became a 'service economy', where more than half of the population

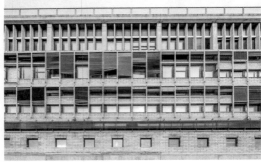

New facade cladding and extensive transformation. In KB32 (2021) Vilhelm Lauritzen Architects breathed new life into DSB's former goods railway building on Kalvebod Brygge in Copenhagen. A good example that reusing existing buildings is also functionalism and much more climate-friendly than demolition.

From a blacksmith's forge to an auditorium with almost ecclesiastical qualities. The Assembly Hall, Auditorium 1 (1861/1995) at the Royal Danish Academy of Fine Arts, Schools of Architecture, Design and Conservation. Originally designed by architect Ferdinand Meldahl.

make their living in the service sector, for example writing architecture books or 'trimming each other's beards', as the Social Liberal politician Viggo Hørup famously put it. This development freed up many industrial buildings, most of which, unlike the housing stock from that era, were not demolished but instead respectfully restored.

That is not surprising, since with the tough realities of industrial production at a comfortable distance, the old industrial buildings, in all their naked functionalism, exude an exotic charm that many associate with the loft studios of post-war New York artists. As lifestyle and home interior magazines know, the 'industrial look' never really goes out of fashion in the romanticism that an increasingly refined and well-furnished civilization will always entertain, out of sheer longing for the kind of experience that had Thoreau leaving for Walden Pond. With retrofitted insulation, the industrial buildings also make excellent workspaces for 'creative professions', as they offer plenty of room and lots of natural daylight through large windows and steep glazed shed roofs.

With the restoration of the Danish Navy's buildings from the second half of the 19th century on Holmen island in Copenhagen, Vilhelm Lauritzen Architects transformed just this type of building into an educational environment for architects. The refurbishment transformed the buildings to the benefit of modern-day users and did so 'with much grace', as it said in the British journal *The Architectural Review*. Vilhelm Lauritzen Architects 'seized the wonderful site with relish and respect. They were required to reflect the buildings' previous uses in their conversions, and their touch has been very light'.[120]

A similarly sensitive and musical but also independently and clearly designed solution has been achieved with the 'rescue operation' (2021) that was carried out to preserve architect Ole Hagen's Brutalist former goods railway building KB32 from 1967. New facade cladding for the neglected concrete building proved a way to uncover the original qualities with limited means by adding something new. By breaking the very long Bernstorffsgade facade into several different compositions or 'musical staffs' made of window frames, the architects recreated the original building rhythm in a new expression, elegant and refined despite the monumental scale. Underneath, the sins of the interim period lie hidden as a mess of expressions that clearly demonstrated why variation alone is not the answer.

'One of the finest facades in Copenhagen in years,' wrote Berlingske's architecture critic Holger Dahl of KB32 after the building's extensive transformation. The 80-metre-long building on Kalvebod Brygge was originally a freight-railway building, built in 1967, but now serves as the offices for the Poul Schmith law firm and the Danish National Archives with a capacity of up to a thousand employees.

You have our attention

Subtle references in Vilhelm
Lauritzen Architects' studio in
Nordhavn exemplified by the
perforated panels that elegantly
(and functionally) point back
to the harlequin pattern at The
People's House.

Vilhelm Lauritzen Architects also practises recycling, restoration or 'revitalization' in its own offices in Nordhavn.

For obvious reasons, no architects can really abide working in a building designed by someone else, and since it is usually prohibitively expensive to build from scratch near the city centre, where architects like to have their offices, most firms arrive at the right solution through renovation. Besides, they also need an office space that showcases their talent and skill to prospective clients.

That is also true of Vilhelm Lauritzen Architects, which, as mentioned, has its base in a former warehouse. When the firm took over the lease, it was still in its raw warehouse state. Keen to preserve that atmosphere, the architects mostly maintained the open-plan structure, sectioned off meeting rooms with glass doors and the service facilities with light gypsum walls, installed Troldtekt acoustic panels in the ceilings and preserved and polished the large existing concrete floor. As a warm contrast to the concrete, the meeting rooms are lined with birch plywood boards with sound-dampening perforations in a discreet harlequin pattern of large triangles.

Out of veneration for the firm's history and its founder, the pattern on the panels at the studio was inspired by the ornamentation inside The People's House. However, while the pattern on the balcony fronts in the Small Hall at The People's House is a fairly dominating decorative statement in the overall expression, its contemporary, toned-down interpretation on the modern-day studio walls is an image of modern architecture in 2022:

You have our attention. We're listening.

The former warehouse that is
now home to Vilhelm Lauritzen
Architects.

Vilhelm Theodor Lauritzen
(1894–1984)

Vilhelm Theodor Lauritzen was one of Denmark's most significant architects in his time and one of the originators of Danish modernism. To this day, many of his projects remain enduring examples of what was then a new and revolutionary architecture in which form follows function. Although few may be aware of it, most Danes have encountered his designs and the works of the architecture firm that continues in his name. From the outset, his goal was to create high-quality architecture for the people. Never one to put himself in the spotlight, his personality only occasionally comes through in texts and images, and even though Lauritzen became one of the principal Danish architects of the 20th century, he had little interest in personal profiling.

Besides architecture, Lauritzen had a lifelong passion for nature, especially butterflies. In 1954, he said in an interview that had he not become an architect with butterflies as his hobby, he would have become a zoologist with drawing as a sideline.[121] Above all, however, he was an architect, and throughout his career he maintained that architecture should be applied art for everyone – not the exclusive reserve of a privileged few. Among Vilhelm Lauritzen's most acclaimed works are Copenhagen Airport's first terminal building, now known as the Vilhelm Lauritzen Terminal, the Radio House in Frederiksberg, the People's House (now VEGA) in Copenhagen and the Danish Embassy in Washington, DC. They all share a characteristic humanistic feel and represent a society that was undergoing rapid transformation in the 20th century.

Space and form across generations

Vilhelm Lauritzen was born on 10 September 1894 in Slagelse; he took his upper secondary exam at Sorø Akademi in 1912 and graduated from the Royal Danish Academy of Fine Arts, School of Architecture in 1921. The following year, he founded Tegnestuen Vilhelm Lauritzen (Studio Vilhelm Lauritzen). Study trips to Spain and Greece had a significant impact on his later work, including his first major project, Daell's Department Store, a competition he won in 1922 in collaboration with architect Frits Schlegel.

His drawings clearly reflect his ideal of designing space and form to last for generations. In order to fully appreciate how groundbreaking his architecture was, we need to consider his work in the context of its time. While architecture had long focused on a building's form and ornamentation, Lauritzen's approach revolved around usability. With a free mindset guided by functionality he created solutions that were so simple and effective their true brilliance might be overlooked at first glance. That was the case, for example, with the first terminal at Copenhagen Airport.

When Lauritzen began the design process in 1936, commercial air travel was still a novel phenomenon, and there were no models for what a commercial airport should look like. In a functionalist approach, he divided the building into airside and landside sections. Entrance and traffic were managed through or along the landside section, while aeroplanes and gates belonged airside. Today, this is still how most airports around the world are designed.

Another example is Lauritzen's design of the Radio House from 1945. Today, it is a listed, internationally acknowledged *Gesamtkunstwerk*, designed without compromise from the inside out – from lamps and furniture to its modernist typology. It is one of the most accomplished examples of functionalist architecture, with its specific functions, such as the foyer, the concert hall and the offices, directly legible in its form. The sound studios function as Chinese boxes, with walls and foundations constructed without parallel walls in order to provide optimal acoustics and sound insulation. The building has an almost touching quality of timelessness and durability and an unusual dedication to detailing and material sensibility. Today, the corridors of the building still resonate with music, now produced by the students at the Royal Danish Academy of Music.

His modernist talent also manifested in interiors and the design of everything from door handles, ashtrays and stair railings to lamps, sofas and chairs. His best-known product design is the Radio House Pendant, which is still in production. Several of his furniture designs were co-created with Finn Juhl, who was employed as an architect in Lauritzen's studio for 11 years, from 1934 to 1945.

As for his personal life, Vilhelm Lauritzen was married to Ingeborg Lauritzen (née Ziegler), who was also an architect. Together, they had a daughter, Ester Sidoroff. He was awarded the Order of Dannebrog, Knight 1st class, in 1941. That same year he was awarded the Eckersberg Medal, in 1954 the C. F. Hansen Medal and in 1964 the honorary medal of the Danish Association of Architects. From 1946 he was a corresponding member of the Royal Institute of British Architects.

Vilhelm Lauritzen retired in 1969 but kept coming into the office for many years after and left behind a firm that continues to preserve and develop the modernist legacy. He passed away in 1984, at the age of ninety.

Although Vilhelm Lauritzen preferred being behind the camera, here he has been captured in the lobby of the ambassador's residence in connection with the official opening of the Danish Embassy in Washington, DC, in 1960.

'I see a tendency to reduce architecture to its own purpose, but that makes it pointless.'

- Vilhelm Lauritzen, 1964

Notes

1 Niels Boserup, *Et modernistisk mesterværk: Arkitekten Vilhelm Lauritzens lufthavnsbygning fra 1939* (A modernist masterpiece: Architect Vilhelm Lauritzen's airport terminal from 1939), Copenhagen 2001.

2 Vilhelm Lauritzen founded Tegnestuen Vilhelm Lauritzen (Studio Vilhelm Lauritzen) in 1922. In 1959, Mogens Boertmann, Helge H. Hoppe and Jørgen Anker Heegaard joined as partners, and in 1962, Lauritzen and his partners founded Vilhelm Lauritzens Tegnestue I/S (Vilhelm Lauritzen's Studio Partnership). In 1964, the partners took over the firm, and Lauritzen continued as a consultant until 1969. In 1971, the company was converted into a private limited company owned by Mogens Boertmann, Jørgen Anker Heegaard, Ole Palm Grupe and Hans Jørgensen. In 1977, the name changed to VLT A/S (VLT Ltd), now owned by Mogens Boertmann, Jens Ammundsen and Svend Erik Ladefoged. In 1979, Medarbejderfonden for VLT A/S (Employee Foundation for VLT Ltd) and in 1981 a VLT A/S Fyns afdeling (VLT Ltd. Funen department) were founded. In 1983, Medarbejderfonden became a co-owner of the firm along with Jens Ammundsen, Svend Erik Ladefoged, Jørn Rohde Nielsen, Flemming Nyberg, Jan Hansen and Christian Holm, while Mogens Boertmann stayed on in an advisory capacity until 1987. In 1989, the name was changed to Vilhelm Lauritzen AS (Vilhelm Lauritzen Ltd) with the partners Svend Erik Ladefoged, Jens Ammundsen, Christian Holm, Flemming Nyberg, Jens Rohde Nielsen, Jan Hansen and Medarbejderfonden. In 2000, Thomas Scheel, Torsten Stephensen and Søren Daugbjerg were included as partners, and the name was changed to the current Vilhelm Lauritzen Architects. Today, the firm is led by a partnership consisting of architects Anne Møller Sørensen, Thomas West Jensen, Thomas Scheel, Torsten Stephensen, Simon Natanael Svensson, Michael Schytt Poulsen, Daniel Illum-Davis, Malte Rosenquist, Jakob Meyling, Jeppe Dueholm, Lasse Herbo Madsen and CEO Gyrithe Saltorp, COO Christian Egedius Bendtsen and the German private equity fund Findos. Sources: Lisbet Balslev Jørgensen, Jørgen Sestoft and Morten Lund, *Vilhelm Lauritzen: A modern architect*, Copenhagen 1994, 333, and Vilhelm Lauritzen Architects.

3 The word 'modern' is not itself all that modern. Known instances of it date back to late antiquity, towards the end of the fifth century CE, whenever some *moderni* wanted to distance themselves from the old *antiqui*, whom they viewed as hopelessly outdated, or, conversely, when antiquity or some other past historical era was held out as superior to the current time. Our perception of the current time as modern owes much to the French poet Baudelaire and his contemporaries, who around 1850 intensively promoted *la modernité* as the slogan of a new contemporary aesthetic for the tempestuously romantic, technologically and politically revolutionary nineteenth century that was unfolding especially in the rapidly urbanizing metropolises of Paris, London and Berlin. See the chapter on modernity in Hans Robert Jauss, *Literaturgeschichte als Provokation* (Literary history as provocation), Frankfurt a.M. 1970. An English translation of Jauss's chapter published in 2005, 'Modernity and literary tradition', can be found in the journal *Critical Inquiry* 31, 2: 329–364. See Baudelaire's aesthetic articulated in, e.g., Charles Baudelaire, 'La peintre de la vie moderne' (The painter of modern life) (1863), in *Oeuvres complétes de Baudelaire*, Paris 1950.

4 Jürgen Habermas, 'Modernity versus postmodernity', *New German Critique* 22, 1981: 3–14.

5 Gregor Paulsson, *Ny svensk arkitektur / New Swedish architecture*, Stockholm 1939, 7.

6 The 'We are' section on the website of Vilhelm Lauritzen Architects: https://vilhelmlauritzen.com/about (accessed June 2022).

7 Personal communication with Thomas Scheel, June 2020.

8 The famous aphorism is attributed to the German architect Ludwig Mies van der Rohe, who himself refers to his colleague and mentor Peter Behrens, Mies's supervisor in the iconic AEG turbine factory (1909) in Berlin's Moabit district. As a work assignment, he presented some proposals for the facade design, to which Behrens allegedly commented, 'Weniger ist mehr' (less is more). See Detlef Mertins, *Mies*, London 2014.

9 Personal communication with Anne Møller Sørensen, June 2020.

10 Mike Rømer, 'Transparent tryghed' (Transparent security), *Arkitekten* 118, 1, 2016: 20–22.

11 Karsten Ifversen, 'Nyt sygehus vender vrangen ud på psykiatrisk behandling' (New hospital turns psychiatric treatment inside out), *Politiken*, 30 August 2015.

12 The Renaissance poet Francesco Petrarch rediscovered the ancient Roman writer Cicero and adopted him as his personal role model, not in accordance with the instruction of the powers that be but on his own autonomous authority. For that reason, Petrarch has been called 'the first modern man'.

13 'If many people read his project description, the competition would not have been fruitless', wrote architect Steen Eiler Rasmussen in his commentary to the competition. Steen Eiler Rasmussen, 'Hanstholm', *Architekten* 26, 1924.

14 Lauritzen's project description according to Rasmussen, 'Hanstholm', 111.

15 Ibid., 110.

16 Ibid., 107.

17 Jørgensen, Sestoft and Lund, *Vilhelm Lauritzen*, 14.

18 The Kronløb Island team includes Vilhelm Lauritzen Architects and Cobe, landscape architects STED and the engineering company Rambøll. The contractor is NCC. The client is Kronløbsøen Projekt P/S (P/S meaning project company), which consists of CPH City & Port Development, the pension fund PensionDanmark and the property development firm Nordkranen.

19 According to architect and partner Rosa Lund, STED, in an interview on the website for Kronløbsbassinet: https://kronlobsbassinet.dk/kronloebsoeen-mimer-den-danske-urskov/ (accessed June 2021).

20 Ibid.

21 Kåre Flindt Jørgensen, NCC, in an interview on the website for Kronløbsbassinet: https://kronlobsbassinet.dk/med-ingenioeren-paa-arbejde/ (accessed June 2021).

22 Ibid.

23 Ibid.

24 A personal recollection. For a number of years, this author worked in Vilhelm Lauritzen's the Radio House. Every morning I rounded the building on the corner of Rosenørns Allé and Julius Thomsens Gade, where the connection between the office wing and the concert hall, in a classic modernistic move, has been pulled slightly back to make room for a small grove of plane trees. Planes have a characteristic fragrance, and whenever I passed by, the smell reminded me of childhood holidays in southern Europe. Thus, every day when I came into work I was going on a holiday, in a sense – in my memory.

25 'Une maison est une machine à habiter, comme un fauteuil est une machine à s'asseoir.' Le Corbusier, *Vers une architecture* (1923), Paris 1977, 73. English translation: *Towards a New Architecture*, London 1931.

26 Emil Kaufmann, *Von Ledoux bis Le Corbusier: Ursprung und Entwicklung der autonomen Architektur* (From Ledoux to Le Corbusier: Origin and development of autonomous architecture), Vienna 1933.

27 For example, the American urban historian Lewis Mumford argued that modernity began in the Middle Ages with the introduction of the printing press and the monastery bells with their regular calls to prayer, as this introduced a man-made method of time-keeping as opposed to natural time, marked by the rising and setting of the sun and the changing of the seasons.

28 Karl Marx's co-author of *The Communist Manifesto*, Friedrich Engels, described how the proletariat of newly arrived workers in London and Manchester 'slept hungry and half-naked in the street', suffering from typhus due to open sewers and the lack of clean water, and how even young children worked 14–16 hours a day and that half of them died before the age of five: 'The proletarian, who has nothing but his two hands, who consumes today what he earned yesterday, […] is placed in the most revolting, inhuman position conceivable for a human being.' Friedrich Engels, *Condition of the Working Class in England* (1887), Panther edn, 1969, unpaginated at https://www.marxists.org/archive/marx/works/download/pdf/condition-working-class-england.pdf (accessed May 2022). Original work published in Leipzig, 1845.

29 According to the 1922 *Statistisk Aarbog* (Statistical Yearbook), on 1 February 1860 Copenhagen had a population of 155,143. By 1 February 1921, that number had reached 561,344, more than 700,000 including suburbs. In just half a century, the Danish population more than doubled, with most of the growth in the cities. In 1860, less than half a million Danes lived in cities. By 1921, the cities had surpassed the country with a population of nearly 1.8 million, compared to less than 1.5 million in the country. Christian Wichmann Matthiessen, *Danske byers vækst: Atlas over Danmark. Serie II bd. 3* (Growth of Danish cities: Atlas of Denmark. Series II, vol. 3), Copenhagen 1985, 22.

30 Henning Bro, 'Oversigt: Boligpolitikkens historie – et upåagtet forskningsområde' (Overview: History of housing policy – a neglected research area), *Historisk Tidsskrift* 106, 2, 2006: 586–613. See also by Bro, *Boligen mellem natvægterstat og velfærdsstat: Bygge- og boligpolitik i tre danske bysamfund, 1850–1930* (Housing: From night watchman state to welfare state: Construction and housing policy in three Danish towns, 1850–1930), PhD dissertation, University of Copenhagen, 2006.

31 Jesper Engelmark, *Københavnsk etageboligbyggeri 1850–1900: En byggeteknisk undersøgelse* (Copenhagen multi-storey housing 1850–1900: A study of building technology), Hørsholm 1983, 54. The main source of infection in unhealthy cities was the water supply. In Copenhagen, as elsewhere, each building originally had its own dug well, but over time the water became unpotable due to contamination from latrines. In 1626, private water utilities were established that pumped water from Emdrup Lake, the moats and Peblinge Lake and led it into the city via wooden pipes. The pipes were not buried deep enough or sufficiently tight to prevent anything from wastewater to rotten plant debris and even small eels from the lakes to enter what was supposed to be drinking water. In the mid 19th century, the streets of Copenhagen were still open sewers, and in 1853 a cholera epidemic in Denmark claimed more than six thousand lives over a few summer months, the vast majority of them in Copenhagen. This epidemic added new momentum to the debate about the connection between housing conditions and public health, as it documented the fatal risks of poor housing – and not just to the people living in such conditions, which undoubtedly added to the sense of urgency. The Danish Medical Association launched an appeal that raised the funds for the first social housing project in Denmark, the Medical Association's Housing Scheme in Østerfælled, Copenhagen.

32 In the book *Garden Cities of Tomorrow* (London 1898), the author, British urban planner Ebenezer Howard, advocated combining social and environmental benefits by building green 'garden cities' with common areas and terrace houses or small detached houses in a coherent architectural expression, all on the scale of a village but intended for industrial and white-collar workers. His ideas soon inspired an influential movement, which also spread to Denmark. One Danish example of the realization of these ideas is Den Engelske Haveby (the English Garden City) in Brønshøj from 1923. The Bauhaus school of architecture and design in Weimar and later in Dessau, Germany, was oriented more towards the conditions of industrial society and its revolutionary influence on all design and production. Several of the leading figures at the Bauhaus, including Walter Gropius and, not least, Hannes Meyer, saw architecture as a key instrument in building a better society.

33 Initially, the 'housing issue' in Denmark, as in other Western European countries mainly attracted philanthropist initiatives, but with the growing, and soon also legal, labour movement and the young Social Democratic Party's strategy of 'municipal socialism', housing gradually became a political issue too. The first law about public subsidies for the construction of housing was passed in 1887, and when the journeyman painter Jens Jensen became Mayor of Copenhagen in 1903, he initiated the construction of municipal housing.

34 The agreement was reached in the private home of Prime Minister Stauning and named after the street where he lived, Kanslergade 10, 1st floor, to the right, in the centre of Copenhagen.

35 Nils-Ole Lund, *Nordic Architecture*, transl. J. Manley, Copenhagen 2008, 246.

36 Designed by two of Lauritzen's former employees: Povl Ernst Hoff and Bennet Windinge.

37 The building system was developed in collaboration with Adserballe & Knudsen as turnkey contractor, Holmsgaard engineers and the landscape architecture firm Thing Brandt Landskab.

38 The squatter's rule in Act no. 227 of 19 May 1971, which changed the Renovation Act's Sec. 55, par. 2 to make it legal for citizens to use and reside in properties that were slated for demolition until such time as they were demolished.

39 Steen Eiler Rasmussen, *Omkring Christiania* (About Christiania), Copenhagen 1976, 17.

40 See John Mogensen's lyrics for the hit song 'Der er noget galt i Danmark' (Something's rotten in Denmark) (1971): 'See what's happening / in the old streets / in the middle of our city, Copenhagen. / Hideous boxes going up, / now the turn has come to our beloved Christianshavn.'

41 L.L. Clausen, 'Der kommer aldrig højhuse på Krøyers Plads', *Berlingske*, 3 February 2011.

42 Personal communication with Thomas Scheel, June 2020.

43 See Københavns Kommune, 'Workshop Krøyers Plads', at https://www.kk.dk/sites/default/files/agenda/e2cfd06e-9049-4228-8588-7c4abe19b4e3/2443c7b5-066f-47b6-b4cd-5d401e0aee75-bilag-3.pdf (accessed May 2022).

44 Karsten R.S. Ifversen, 'Christianshavnere vil selv bestemme over omstridt grund' (Christianshavn residents want to make their own decisions about disputed site), *Politiken*, 19 April 2011.

45 GHB was the landscape architect for the project, and NCC both the client and the contractor.

46 Interview with Thomas Scheel and others in Mads Elsøe and Maja Langberg, 'Tag en gåtur ved havnen: Tre tegnestuer fortæller, hvad du skal lægge mærke til' (Advertisement for Danish Architecture Center), *Politiken*, 15 September 2020.

47 Vilhelm Lauritzen, 'Nogle Arbejder for Gladsaxe Kommune' (Some work for Gladsaxe Municipality), *Arkitekten* 43, 8, 1941: 125.

48 Jørgensen, Sestoft and Lund, *Vilhelm Lauritzen*, 69 ff.

49 Ibid., 88.

50 Niels Hesse, 'Det fuldmurede etagehus' (The brick-built high-rise), *Tegl* 102, 4, 1999: 20–21.

51 Ibid.

52 Alvar Aalto in Kenneth Frampton, *Modern Architecture*, Kindle edn, London 1980, 415.

53 According to Vilhelm Lauritzen Architects' project presentation at vla.dk: https://vilhelmlauritzen.com/da/collection-of-work/nyt-hospital-nordsjaelland/ (accessed May 2022).

54 According to Vilhelm Lauritzen Architects' project presentation at vla.dk: https://www.vla.dk/project/nyt-hospital-nordsjaelland/ (accessed August 2021).

55 Vilhelm Lauritzen Architects, *Udvalgte projekter* (Selected projects), ed. Thomas Scheel and Søren Daugbjerg, Copenhagen n.d., 227.

56 Ibid., 228.

57 Ibid.

58 Ibid.

59 Adolf Loos, 'Ornament and crime' (1908), in Ulrich Conrads (ed.), *Programs and Manifestoes on 20th-Century Architecture*, Cambridge, MA, 1975.

60 Vilhelm Lauritzen, 'Forslag til nyt Zoologisk Museum paa Nørre Fælled' (Proposal for new zoological museum at Nørre Fælled), *Arkitekten* 33, 6, 1931: 112.

61 Louis Henry Sullivan, 'The tall office building artistically considered', *Lippincott's Magazine*, April 1896: 406–409.

62 Eugène Emmanuel Viollet-le-Duc, *Discourses on Architecture* (1863–72), transl. H. Van Brunt, Boston 1875, 172–184.

63 Ellen Stegmann and Hother Stegmann (eds.), *Povl Stegmann: 1888–1944*, Ringkøbing 1953, 39. Quoted from Jørgensen, Sestoft and Lund, *Vilhelm Lauritzen*, 9.

64 Lund, *Nordic Architecture*, 20.

65 Jørgensen 1994, 10.

66 Ibid., 11.

67 Ibid., 18.

68 Hans Erling Langkilde, 'Vilhelm Lauritzen 70 år' (Vilhelm Lauritzen, 70 years), *Arkitekten* 66, 18, 1964: 364.

69 Jørgensen, Sestoft and Lund, *Vilhelm Lauritzen*, 22.

70 One of the most influential institutions in modern architecture is the Bauhaus school of architecture and crafts, founded in 1919 by the German architect Walter Gropius and closed down by the Nazis in 1933. The teaching staff included some of the most significant modern architects and artists, among them Ludwig Mies van der Rohe, Paul Klee and Wassily Kandinsky. On par with Le Corbusier, Bauhaus is the essence of functionalism. The name of the Bauhaus school and Lyonel Feininger's woodcut on the cover of the school's first manifesto refer to the notion that even the greatest art, exemplified in this case by Gothic cathedrals, was created by craftsmen, whose sheds, *Bauhütten* in German, lie at the foot of the cathedral, bathed in the light of the guiding stars of art. Craftsmanship is the art that builds civilizations, and the industrial culture is merely a tool of this building task – albeit the most efficient tool ever. Hence, the modern architect is building society, not just houses, and construction, buildings, city, space, the built environment – *der Bau* – is the foundation of civilization.

71 Vilhelm Lauritzen, 'Nørrebros Teater', *Arkitekten* 34, 19, 1932.

72 Jørgensen, Sestoft and Lund, *Vilhelm Lauritzen*, 45.

73 Ibid., 54.

74 'The Wooden Castle [...] had the look of a summer camp, with the trim wooden building symmetrically placed behind a circular lawn with a flagpole in the middle.' Sestoft in Jørgensen, Sestoft and Lund, *Vilhelm Lauritzen*, 121.

75 Ibid.

76 Latin conveys the seriousness of the matter. 'Gravity' comes from the Latin word *gravitas*, meaning seriousness, and *gravis*, meaning heavy. Gravity pulls us down, and everything that we are carrying with us, including ourselves, is a burden that reminds us that there is also a *grave* somewhere – a word, by the way, that seems to have roots in the earliest beginnings of language. We are the very weight that weighs us down, and we are only liberated from it when we are in our grave. On the other hand, we literally would not have a leg to stand on were it not for gravity. Nor would architecture have a chance if it could not stand upright.

77 Sestoft in Jørgensen, Sestoft and Lund, *Vilhelm Lauritzen*, 124.

78 'Til Paris på seks timer' (To Paris in six hours), *Politiken*, 19 September 1925, 8.

79 Sestoft in Jørgensen, Sestoft and Lund, *Vilhelm Lauritzen*, 185.

80 Ibid., 189.

81 Quoted from Sestoft in Jørgensen, Sestoft and Lund, *Vilhelm Lauritzen*, 150.

82 Svend Erik Møller, 'Trappe op, trappe ned' (Going up stairs, going down stairs), *Politiken*, 8 July 1960, 9–10.

83 Poul Erik Skriver ['Skr'], 'Ridderslaget' (Knighted), *Arkitekten* 62, 15, 1960: 249.

84 Langkilde, 'Vilhelm Lauritzen 70 år', and caption for the accompanying photo of Copenhagen Airport, Terminal 2.

85 Anthony Vidler, *Histories of the immediate present: Inventing architectural modernism*, Cambridge, MA, 2008.

86 Kaufmann, *Von Ledoux bis Le Corbusier*. See also by Kaufmann 'Die Stadt des Architekten Ledoux: Zur Erkenntnis der autonomen Architektur' (The city of the architect Ledoux: On the realisation of autonomous architecture) in the journal *Kunstwissenschaftliche Forschungen* 2, 1933: 131–160.

87 Note the past tense. This was written during the Covid pandemic, which turned (especially) air travel upside down. In the case of Copenhagen Airport, the passenger numbers for 2020 shot down to the level of 1970. At the time of writing, it remains unclear whether travel habits have changed for good, out of fear of infection, or whether air travel will rebound to its pre-pandemic levels.

88 Morten Lund, 'Fredning-flytning: En bygning, der repræsenterer vor egen tids begyndelse' (Listing – relocation: A building that represents the beginnings of our own time), *Arkitektur- og byggebladet ada*, November 1995: 14–16.

89 DR-TV, *Det ny DR* (The new DR), TV programme, 5 March 2006.

90 'Arkitekter vil være digitale frontløbere' (Architects want to be digital front-runners), *Dansk Industri Business*, 27 October 2020.

91 Published 1751–72. In English: *Encyclopedia, or a Systematic Dictionary of the Sciences, Arts, and Crafts*.

92 Immanuel Kant, 'An answer to the question: What is enlightenment? (1784)' in *The collected works of Immanuel Kant: Practical philosophy*, transl. and ed. Mary J. Gregor, Cambridge, UK, 1996, 17.

93 Personal communication with Torsten Stephensen, June 2020.

94 A.S. Neill, *Summerhill: A radical approach to child-rearing*, London 1960, 5.

95 Personal communication with Torsten Stephensen, June 2020.

96 Ibid.

97 Søren Præstholm, Anne Gravsholt Busck and Søren Bech Pilgaard Kristensen, 'Landskab og byudvikling: Analyse af kommuneplanlægning og samspil mellem planaktører i Roskilde Kommune' (Landscape and urban development: Analysis of municipal planning and interaction among planning actors in Roskilde Municipality), Working Paper 21, University of Copenhagen, 2011, 47.

98 Personal communication with Torsten Stephensen, June 2020.

99 'Anordning for Almue-Skolevæsenet paa Landet i Danmark, 29. juli 1814' (Directive for rural school services in Denmark, 29 July 1814), in *Kong Frederik den Siettes allernaadigste Forordninger og aabne Breve for Aar 1814*, 1814, 237–264.

100 'Lov om Folkeskolen' (Act on municipal primary and lower secondary education), *Lovtidende* 160, 1937, 866–884.

101 Jean-Jacques Rousseau, *Émile, or On Education* (1763), transl. Barbara Foxley, New York 2020, 2.

102 Ibid., 4.

103 *Das ganz Andere* – the entirely other – is the German philosopher Theodor W. Adorno's little window-left-ajar of a utopian perspective seen in light of human civilization's domination of nature, which leads to a coercive domination of humanity itself, manifested by the division of labour and a host of other social and individual mechanisms of restraint and self-restraint. Only the arts, according to Adorno, contain such a window in an otherwise completed 'administered world'.

104 Stanley Cavell, *The senses of Walden*, Chicago 1972, 86.

105 Henry David Thoreau, *Walden; Or life in the woods* (1845), Stilwell, KS, 2005, 8–9.

106 Ibid., 11.

107 Ibid., 35.

108 Ibid., 88.

109 Personal communication with Simon Natanael Svensson, June 2020.

110 Ibid.

111 According to Vilhelm Lauritzen Architects' project presentation at vla.dk: https://www.vla.dk/project/europaskolen/ (accessed August 2021).

112 Ibid.

113 Tomas Transtromer, 'Vermeer', in *The Half-Finished Heaven: Selected Poems*, Minneapolis 2017.

114 Sigfried Giedion, 'The dangers and advantages of luxury', *Focus* 1, 3, 1939: 34–39.

115 CIAM (Congrès International d'Architecture Modern, in English: International Congresses of Modern Architecture) was a series of influential international architecture conferences held from 1928 to 1959 with prominent participants, such as Le Corbusier, Walter Gropius, Hendrik Berlage, Gerrit Rietveld, Louis Kahn, Ralph Erskine, Alison and Peter Smithson and Kenzo Tange, among others.

116 Terkel Grum-Schwensen, 'Som smeltende isbjerge' (Like melting icebergs), *Byggeri* 4, 2010.

117 The Danish representation in Mozambique was closed in 2016, and the building now serves as a joint embassy for Germany, Norway and Iceland.

118 See Birgitte Kleis, 'Kork som facademateriale' (Cork as facade material), *Arkitekten* 122, 7, 2020: 103–104.

119 Pixel is based on 'pics', an abbreviation of 'pictures', and 'element', and refers to the smallest elements, or the atoms, of a picture – the small squares that electronic images are broken down to when they are transferred as electric impulses. The image pixelates when we zoom in or when the transfer is slow. The phenomenon was only too familiar in the early computer age, when a computer user sometimes had to spend a long time waiting for a blurry image to turn into a recognizable image on the screen. The principle is similar to a raster, a screen imposed on a photograph when it was reproduced in print. The raster was visible as tiny black and white dots when a newspaper photo was studied through a magnifying glass. Raster comes from the Latin word *rastrum*, meaning to rake, or scraped, and that is exactly how the facade of Trælasthuset appears: raked, scraped, fragmented, frozen, captured in a passing moment.

120 Peter Davey, 'Architectural moves', *Architectural Review* 12, 1998: 51 ff.

121 Lisbet Balslev Jørgensen, Jørgen Sestoft and Morten Lund, *Vilhelm Lauritzen: A modern architect*, Copenhagen 1994, 9.

Index

Illustrations

© Federico Covre – 74t, 121t

© Jens Markus Lindhe / VISDA – 16, 22, 29b, 31, 85t, 89b, 154, 160b, 167m, 167b

© Ludwig Mies van der Rohe / VISDA – 15b

Adam Mørk + Hampus Berndtson – 170m, 170b, 204b, 206

AERO – 71t

akg-images / Manuel Cohen – 39

Bauhaus-Archiv Berlin – 119

Bauhaus Dessau Foundation / Photo: Tenschert, Yvonne, 2011 – 15m

Bruno Schleiffer – 70m

Byhistorisk Samling og Arkiv i Høje-Taastrup – 51

Carl Hansen & Søn / Photo: Enok Holsegård – 178t, 178b

Carl Hansen & Søn / Photo: Mikkel Mortensen / Stylist: Pernille Vest – 179t, 179b

Casper Højer – 157t

Casper Højer – 189, 191b, 195

Copenhagen Museum – 54, 59

Creative Commons – 116

Danish National Art Library – 82, 83t, 84t, 84m, 93, 94m, 94b, 95b, 101b, 117, 120, 122–123, 124t, 125–127, 129, 133, 146, 194t

Deepshikha Jain – 171t, 171m, 226–227

Emil Palmgren/Ritzau Scanpix – 58m

Engineer Gunnar Hjort – 88m

Erik Hansen – 70b

Focus Lighting – 156b

H. L. Hansen (Politiken) – 88t

Heidelberg University Library – 70t

Herzog & De Meuron and Vilhelm Lauritzen Architects – 74m, 75, 182, 229

Historic American Buildings Survey (Library of Congress) – 118

J. Schou – 102bm

Jakob Holmqvist – 72, 103b

Jens Frederiksen, 104, 105t, 106–108, 109t, 234b

Jesper Ray Manlay – 26–27

Jonas Børglum – 173t, 177t

Kontraframe – 55, 56-57, 171b

Lars Hansen / Ritzau Scanpix – 242

Laura Stamer – 46–47, 172b

Lone Mengel – 102b

Louis Poulsen – 104t

Mads Frederik – 53

Marcel Schwarz – 173m

Marcus Bredt – 15t

Marie-Louise Høstbo – 121b

Mini Wolff/Ritzau Scanpix – 58b

Politikens Pressefoto – 71m

Rasmus Hjortshøj – 6–9, 17–19, 36, 42, 62, 64–68, 76, 77t, 77m, 78–79, 90–92, 95m, 96–97, 109b, 110m, 110b, 111t, 134–137, 143–145, 151, 158b, 159m, 160m, 161t, 164t, 166, 167t, 168–169, 172t, 172m, 174t, 174m, 175–176, 177b, 186, 196–203, 204t, 205, 207t, 208–211, 216, 219–220, 232, 234t, 235–241

Robert C. Lautman – 100

Robert P. Ruschak – 37

Rune Buch – 12, 86t, 87b, 130–131

seier+seier – 48

Sjavit Maestro – 49, 85b, 173br

Thomas Scheel – 61

Thomas Schytt Poulsen – 148–149, 156t, 157b, 159t, 160t, 161b, 163, 165b, 225, 233

Tobias Faber – 94t

Unknown photographer – 29t, 83b, 87t, 98–99, 101t, 102t, 103t, 103m, 105b, 114, 139–140, 147, 158t, 162, 164b, 165t, 194m, 207bm, 212–213, 191t, 218

Vagn Guldbrandsen – 88b

Verein der Freunde der Weissenhofsiedlung e.V. – 124b

Vilhelm Theodor Lauritzen – 84b, 85m, 128

Vilhelm Lauritzen Architects – 86b, 89t, 102m, 110t, 111m, 111b, 141, 155, 159b, 170t, 174b, 178m, 179m, 181b, 183, 190, 222–224, 228, 230–231, 243

Vilhelm Lauritzen Architects / Danish National Art Library – 14

Vilhelm Lauritzen Architects and Cobe – 33–35, 173bl, 180, 181t, 181m

Wikimedia Commons – 207b

Ökand / ArkDes – 24

Aage Strüwing – 95t

The publisher has attempted to trace, clear and credit all copyrights for featured illustrations. Should there be any errors or omissions, we invite copyright holders to get in touch, and they will be remunerated as if a prior agreement had been made.

100 Years of Danish Modern – Vilhelm Lauritzen Architects
© 2022 The author and Strandberg Publishing

Publishing editors
Louise Haslund-Christensen, Marianne Krogh
and Jakob Rabe Petersen

Image editing
Claudia Rebecca Juul Kassentoft and Jakob Rabe Petersen

Translation
Dorte Herholdt Silver

Copy editing
Wendy Brouwer

Graphic layout and cover design
Troels Faber – NR2154

Cover photo
Rasmus Hjortshøj – COAST

The book is set in Helvetica Neue LT & Chronicle Text

Paper
Munken Print White 18 115g
Arctic Volume White 150g
Cradle to Cradle Certified®

Image processing
Narayana Press, Gylling

Printing and binding
Narayana Press

Printed in Denmark, 2022
1st edition, 1st print run
ISBN: 978-87-92596-17-8

Strandberg Publishing A/S
Gammel Mønt 14
1117 Copenhagen K
www.strandbergpublishing.dk

Narayana Press keeps track of its environmental impact and CO_2
emission and continuously works towards a more sustainable
production. Narayana Press is certified according to the following
standards: ISO 14001, Nordic Swan Ecolabel, FSC, PEFC and
ClimateCalc. The environmental impact can be calculated for the
individual printed matter and it can be labeled with the resulting
CO_2 emission and the relevant logos.

Printed matter
5041 0562